Atlantic Reef Corals

A HANDBOOK OF THE COMMON

Atlantic

REEF AND SHALLOW-WATER CORALS

Reef

OF BERMUDA, THE BAHAMAS, FLORIDA,

Corals

THE WEST INDIES, AND BRAZIL

F. G. Walton Smith

UNIVERSITY OF MIAMI PRESS
Coral Gables, Florida

First printing, 1948

Third printing, 1976
Library of Congress Catalog Card Number 75-125663
ISBN 0-87024-179-6

Designed by Mary Lipson

Manufactured in the United States of America

Contents

Plates

Figures

Preface

THE CORALS of the warm, shallow seas of the western Atlantic shores have always been of interest to the general public for they are among the most beautiful and spectacular animals of the tropical seas. The shores of Bermuda, South Florida, the Bahamas, West Indies, and the western Atlantic coast as far south as Brazil generally abound with a variety of coral species. Corals interest the scientist for many reasons; they not only present many fascinating problems in physiology and structure but also relate importantly to the surrounding environment. Many of our carbonate rocks are composed principally of such microscopic animals as foraminifera and coccoliths, whose activities millions of years ago produced the great limestone cliffs and chalk hills that exist in many parts of the world today. Corals, however, are the most spectacular rock builders of all. For this reason they are quite as interesting to the geologist as to the marine biologist and oceanographer.

To study living corals it is first of all necessary to distinguish between the bewildering number of species.

Since most authoritative publications in this field are written by specialists from a purely taxonomic point of view, persons working in the tropical western Atlantic need a collected account of the corals, with simple directions for their rapid identification in the field as well as in the laboratory.

It is hoped that the requirements of both scientific and amateur readers have been met. Care has been taken to illustrate this guide with photographs, since these are not only helpful in the rapid identification of specimens but also serve to show the beauty of design inherent in coral structure. This second edition includes a few additional species and illustrations not provided in the original edition. The identification key has been revised. It also includes certain information on the origin of coral reefs not previously available.

Grateful acknowledgment is made of the kindness of the late Dr. Wayland Vaughan and Dr. John Wells in giving advice on taxonomic matters, and of the generous help given by the late Mr. C. S. Daniels in the first edition. Thanks are also gratefully accorded for the efforts of the faculty members and students who have helped collect the corals in the schools's reference collection from which most of the photographic illustrations in this book were made. For the photograph of *Meandrina brasiliensis* we are indebted to Mr. Frank Lyman, who kindly loaned his specimen for the purpose. Thanks are also due to Dr. F. M. Bayer, Dr. Lowell P. Thomas, Mr. Terence M. Thomas, and Dr. Cesare Emiliani for their assistance in preparing the second edition.

F. G. Walton Smith

1

Distribution of Coral Reefs throughout the World

CORAL REEFS are found in many parts of the tropical seas, where they form barriers just beneath the surface of the water and hence present a hidden menace to navigation. They are most beautiful when observed on a calm day, especially if one is able to peer down at them through a glass-bottomed boat or bucket, or through the glass faceplate of shallow-water diving equipment. Some corals form large boulders covered with intricate patterns traced in green and gold. Others form tree-like growths, fancifully resembling antlers of deer or elk. Smaller corals grow between these and appear as multicolored flowers, among which wander brightly colored tropical fish.

On other days, when the ocean is not calm and the reefs not easily seen, the sharp edges of the coral can be a menace, especially to a careless navigator. The West Indian reefs are replete with wrecks, many dating back to the days of the Spanish treasure fleets. Although hidden today by a heavy overgrowth of coral, some of these fabulous prizes still show their presence by an occasional doubloon or gold ornament washed up on the beach.

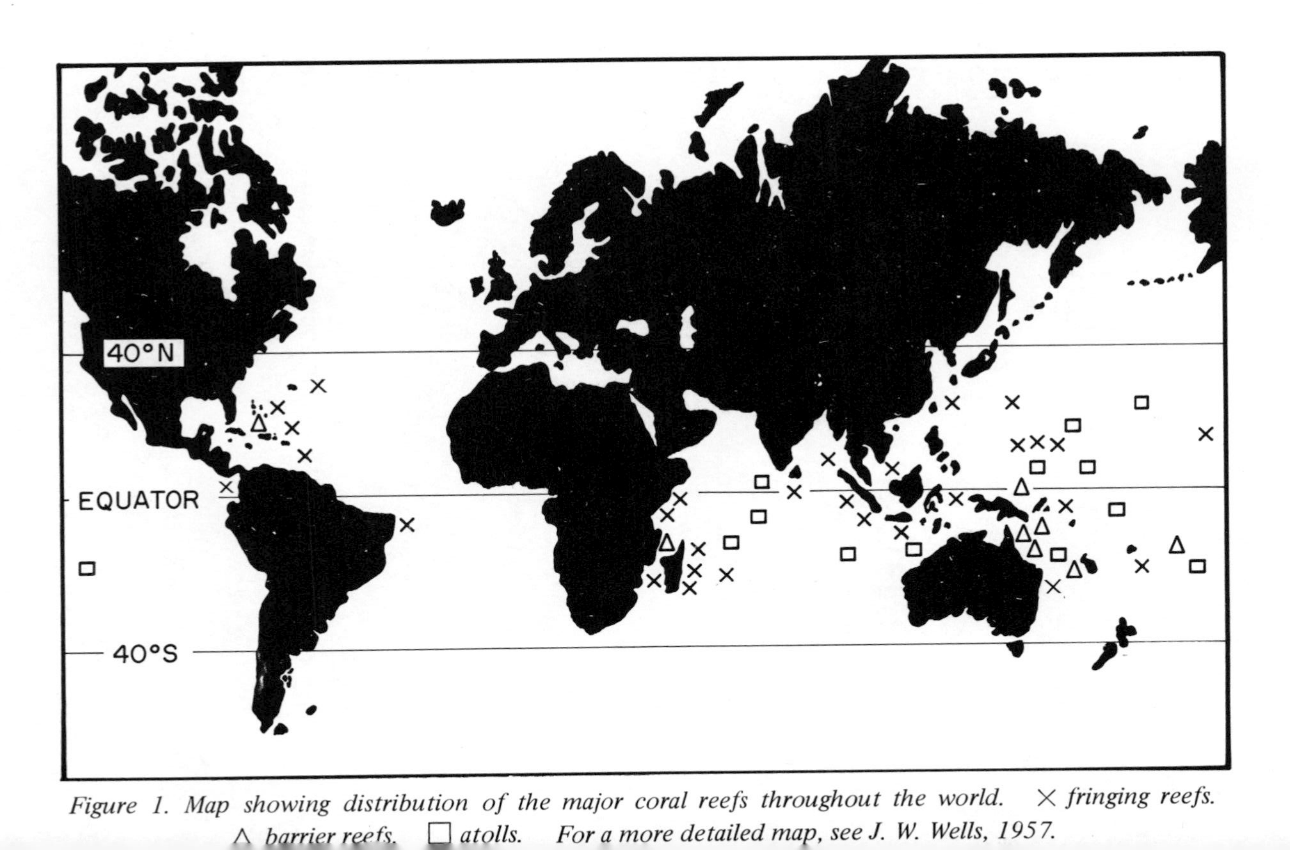

Figure 1. Map showing distribution of the major coral reefs throughout the world. × fringing reefs. △ barrier reefs. □ atolls. For a more detailed map, see J. W. Wells, 1957.

Corals are by no means restricted to the tropics. Certain of them are present in every ocean in shallow depths while others are found in great depths far from shore. They may even be dredged from the cold seas lying within the Arctic and Antarctic Circles. For instance, a delicate branching coral with orange colored fleshy "flowers" on its interwoven twigs has been dredged from a depth of over one thousand feet in the water of the Norwegian fjords. Along the rocky shores of the United States, Canada, and the coasts of England and France, simple corals in the form of tiny individual cups are found. None of these cold-water corals, however, grows so actively or to such a size as the larger reef corals of the tropics. Their form is usually, though not always, small and delicate rather than large and massive. Although a few of these are occasionally found associated with coral reefs, they are not considered to be true reef corals, as a rule.

True reef corals, which individually may reach a size of as much as 35 feet across, are those which are found in fairly shallow depths near tropical shores but never in great depths or in cold water. Even in the tropics they are not found universally, but only in certain well-defined areas. These areas are situated within a belt roughly bounded by the Tropics of Cancer and Capricorn, imaginary lines which are drawn around the earth 23 $1/2^{\circ}$ north and south of the equator and which mark the northern and southern limit of the sun's movement during the year (Fig. 1). Within this 3000 mile-wide belt, coral reefs are abundant on the eastern shores of the Americas, Africa, and Australia, but they are far less common off the western shores of these continents. California and western Mexico have no extensive reef formations similar to those mentioned above. The west coast of Africa is also free of these dangerous but beautiful outgrowths of the ocean floor.

This distribution results from the definite ecological requirements of the individual coral species and a very definite pattern in the occurrence of these desirable conditions throughout the world.

One of the major requirements of reef corals is that the temperature of the surrounding seawater should lie within a range of from 16° to 36° Centigrade (or 61° to 97° Fahrenheit). Most active reef growth takes place within a much narrower range. Exposure to temperatures outside of this range eventually results in the death of reef corals.

The areas where reef corals are best able to flourish are in tropical zones with seawater temperatures ranging from 23° to 25° Centigrade (73° to 77° Fahrenheit). In the Northern Hemisphere ocean currents are forced into a clockwise circular movement by the earth's rotation and associated wind distribution. The opposite is true in the Southern Hemisphere. As a result, warm water travels toward the poles along the eastern shores of the continents. On these shores, therefore, there is a much wider extension of warm water suitable for vigorous coral growth. On the western shores, the reverse is true. Cold currents running toward the equator, combined with upwellings of cold water from the depths, greatly restrict the extent of shoreline favorable to coral growth. Thus it is that reefs are for the most part formed only upon the eastern shores of continents and in the open tropical seas.

While some corals are perfectly capable of living under a small sediment cover, true reef corals are easily killed by mud or sand settling upon them. Corals of the massive boulder type are frequently found dead on the upper surface where sediment naturally collects, while still growing on the outer edge and sides. In extreme cases this may result in the growth of a doughnut-shaped boulder.

Although an animal, the reef coral always contains

within itself algae or small plant-like cells. Plants require light in order to live, and it is believed that the oxygen produced by the algae is necessary for optimum coral growth. Because of this, reef corals and their associated algae are able to flourish in strong sunlight only.

The living coral is a carnivorous animal feeding upon small floating or swimming creatures that it captures by means of stinging tentacles and by means of a slimy secretion of its skin. Since the coral is unable to move in search of food, it must be exposed to water currents or wave action that will bring food to it.

The salinity of seawater is important to corals. Salts in ocean water are in a concentration of about 35 parts per thousand. When this is reduced to less than 25 parts per thousand, reef corals begin to suffer. Similarly, an increase of salinity to 40 is harmful to many corals.

Because sunlight is rapidly absorbed as it passes through seawater, the requirement of strong sunlight restricts reef building to depths less than 150 feet, and vigorous growth to within 90 feet of the surface. The need of water currents to bring food and of wave action to provide oxygenation are also involved in restricting vigorous reef growth to these depths. In deeper water, where wave action and currents are less effective or absent, growth of reef corals is prevented.

The adverse effect of sediment is most pronounced in sheltered water. In shallow water near the shore, there is also likely to be excessive evaporation leading to unduly high salinity, or land drainage of fresh water resulting in dangerously low salinity. These factors, together with the need for wave action, restrict vigorous reefs to the windward side of shorelines and to the seaward side of the reef where heavy seas are pounding.

2

Formation of Coral Reefs

ALTHOUGH all coral reefs are built by the growth and accumulation of the stony skeletons of coral animals, they are not by any means all the same in general appearance and structure. There are, in fact, three main types of reefs. Fringing reefs are found adjacent to the shores of continents or rocky islands in shallow water. In contrast, barrier reefs are separated from the shore by channels of varying width and depth. The third type, known as an atoll, is not connected with any land mass but rises to the surface as a low island, roughly circular in shape and surrounded by deep water.

Fringing reefs are formed by corals growing close to the shore in shallow water. As they increase in size and number, they grow toward the surface and outward toward the open ocean, since water conditions are more favorable in this direction than between the reef and the shore, where conditions of increased temperature, salinity changes, and sediment deposition prevail. The net result of growth at the outer edge of the reef is shown in Fig. 2. A broad platform of partly dead coral rock is formed,

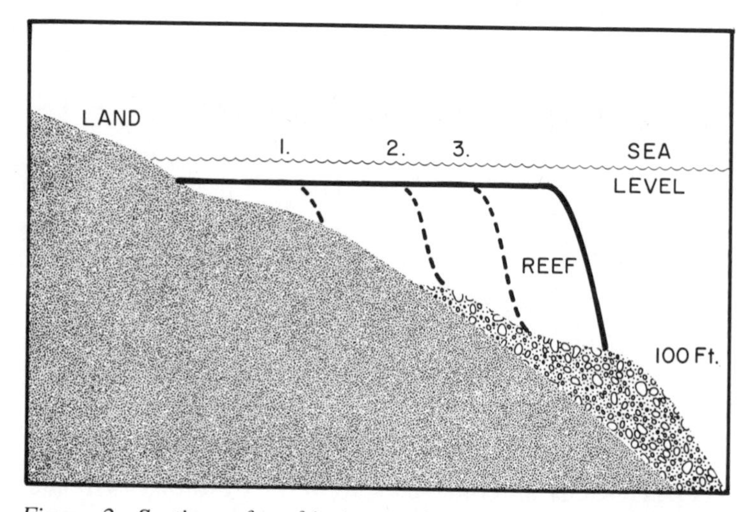

Figure 2. Section of a fringing reef, illustrating the manner of development. Broken lines show successive stages of growth. The living coral does not grow vigorously below 100 feet. Seaward extension of the reef is therefore dependent upon coral broken by wave action rolling to the foot and building up a base of dead rock to a sufficiently shallow depth for growth to occur. Simplified and not to scale.

extending horizontally from the shore. The living and actively growing part of the reef at the seaward edge slopes steeply downward. The edge of this type of reef is separated from the land by very shallow water, and at low tides the entire reef platform may be exposed. Unless large-scale movements of the land or sea level take place, the reef is limited in its seaward extension to a point where its base has reached a depth of about 90 feet. Beyond this, vigorous coral growth cannot take place. A certain amount of seaward extension may take place, however, as the result of broken coral rolling down to the foot and building up a base of dead rock upon which new growth may occur.

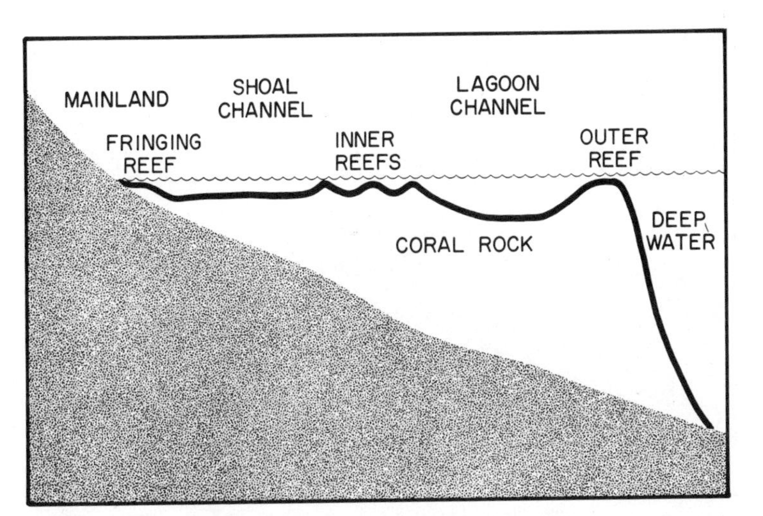

Figure 3. Sections of a barrier reef. After Jukes. Not to scale. The reef grows outward from the land. When the sea floor becomes too deep for vigorous coral growth, the reef may continue to develop upon the talus or coral fragments that build up a foundation for it beyond the seaward edge.

Fringing reefs are found on the shores of the east coast of Africa, Madagascar, Java, the Solomon Islands and the Carolines, with isolated occurrences in the West Indies. Poorly developed reefs of this type also occur in Hawaii. The reefs of Florida and the West Indies have been described as fringing reefs, but they differ in many respects and are by no means typical. Therefore, they will be considered separately in the next chapter.

Barrier reefs present an entirely different appearance, and they are both complex and extensive. The most striking example is the Great Barrier Reef of Australia, which has been well described by Yonge (1930) and others. The Great Barrier Reef consists essentially of a line of reefs running parallel to the coastline of northeastern

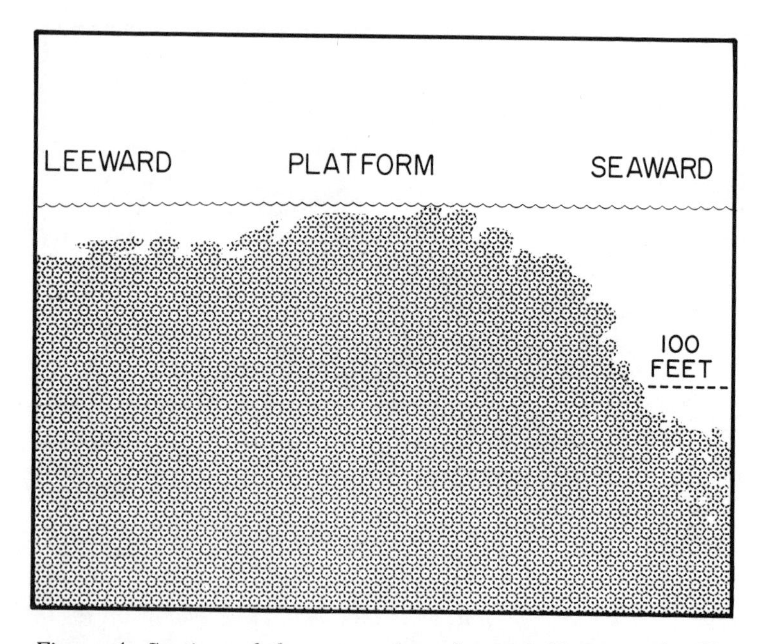

Figure 4. Section of the outer edge of a reef. Not to scale. This indicates a fairly level platform immediately inside the seaward edge, which is relatively continuous. In the deeper water behind this, corals grow in more or less isolated groups.

Australia. It is separated from the mainland by a lagoon channel that is as much as 100 miles wide and 180 feet deep in some places.

The outer or seaward edge of the barrier reef slopes rapidly to a depth of 5000 feet or more within a few miles. Barrier reefs are not always continuous, but they form a more or less broken series of roughly parallel ramparts that are divided into an outer and an inner series (Fig. 3). The latter encroaches more or less into the lagoon channel. The outer edge of each reef has an enormous mass of coral growing just below the surface, forming huge boulders and pinnacles (Fig. 4). These extend seaward under the breakers, constructing a steep, rough cliff that merges below the zone of active growth into a slope of dead coral rock, known as the talus slope. The crevices and gullies within the main platform behind the outer edge of the reef become filled with coral fragments broken off by storm waves. To the lee of the reef, the rock interstices become filled with sand and with small growing corals and coralline algae that cement themselves to the substrate, forming a crude pavement or platform. This pavement is bordered to the leeward by the lagoon channel, which is dotted with scattered heads of coral, various species of algae, foramini-fera, sea grasses, sponges, and gorgonians able to survive in the quieter water behind the main reef platform. The coral heads of this zone become more infrequent toward land, where the effects of fresh-water drainage and suspended sediment become more pronounced. The more exposed parts of the mainland and islands within the lagoon channel often acquire fringing reefs. Small islands may appear on the reef itself as a result of the accumulation of dead coral from storm waves. They often become popu-lated with mangroves and palm trees from seeds washed ashore.

The foregoing brief and simplified description of the Great Barrier Reef applies in a general way to all barrier reefs. These are found in the Pacific among the Society Islands, the Fiji Islands, New Caledonia, and to the southeast of New Guinea, but they are unusual in the Atlantic Ocean and only appear to a limited extent in the Indian Ocean.

Atolls are in many ways the most interesting reef formations, being the true coral islands of romantic fiction as well as of scientific texts. Far from any mainland, they

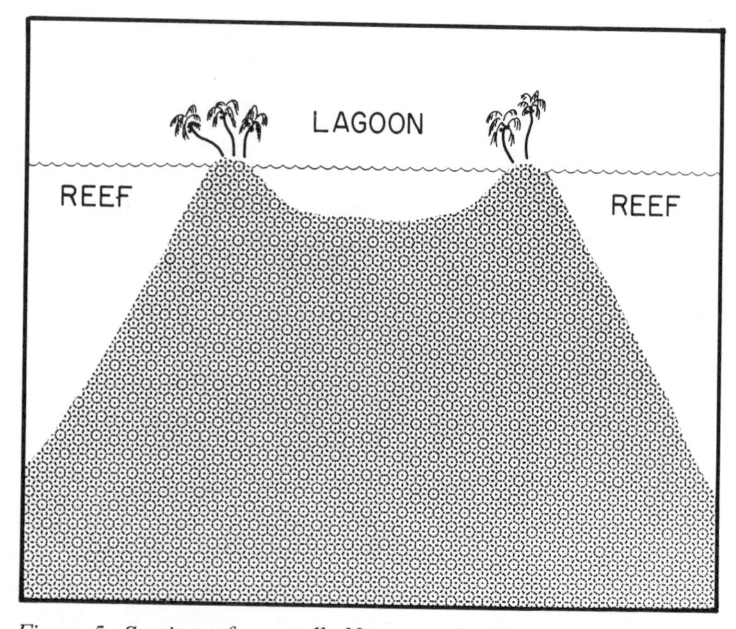

Figure 5. Section of an atoll. Not to scale. The palm trees, which are grossly exaggerated, serve to indicate the formation of islets.

are like oases on the surface of the ocean, arising as if by magic in water thousands of feet deep. Graceful palm trees grow on the fringe of the quiet waters of their protected lagoons where an abundant supply of seafood awaits the hungry castaway. Atolls are of no less interest to the scientist because of their diverse structures and modes of formation. The coral reef of an atoll is essentially similar to that of a barrier reef or fringing reef, but it differs in being roughly circular in shape, with steep outer sides sloping down into very deep water. Inside the encircling ring of reefs is a shallow lagoon that rarely reaches a depth of 100 feet (Figs. 5 and 6). The leeward sides of the reefs lining the lagoon are built up into a series of sand banks

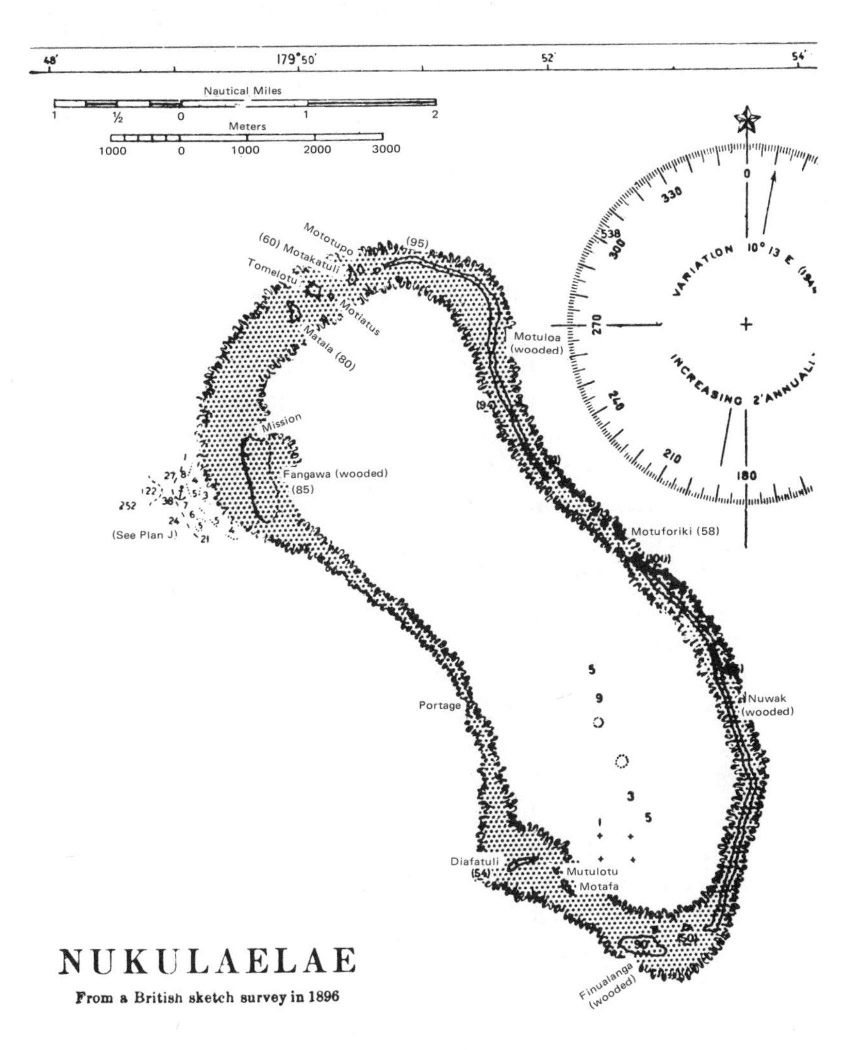

Figure 6. Chart of Nukulaelae, an atoll in the Ellice Island group, South Pacific. From Hydrographic Office Chart No. 1981.

and small islets, which together form a circular island interrupted by gaps that provide access from the ocean to the lagoon. These islets may have some soil and may be covered with vegetation, particularly coconut palms, the large seeds or nuts of which are able to drift thousands of miles across the ocean without losing their ability to germinate.

One of the most typical atolls is the Cocos-Keeling Atoll, situated in the open ocean more than 500 miles from land and surrounded by water more than 6000 feet deep. It was first studied by Charles Darwin in 1836 during the voyage of H.M.S. *Beagle* and, subsequently, by many scientists interested in coral formation. Among these was Wood Jones who, in his book *Corals and Atolls,* described the influence of winds and currents in molding the shape of atolls.

In early times corals were considered a kind of plant, and it was not until 1753 that J. A. de Peysonell, after making a particular study of the western Atlantic reefs, was able to establish conclusively that they are, in fact, a form of animal life. Once this fact was accepted, scientists who followed the early navigators to the tropical seas began to take a great interest in the manner whereby such creatures were able to build atolls, barrier reefs, and fringing reefs. The great difficulty was to explain the appearance of atolls in the middle of deep oceans. At one time it was thought that corals grew at the bottom of the deep tropical seas and that succeeding generations, growing upon the accumulated dead limestone skeletons of their ancestors, would in the course of millions of years reach the surface. Such ideas, however, were soon dispelled by dredging operations that showed quite clearly that reef corals were unable to live and grow except in relatively shallow water. Darwin, in his celebrated book *The Structure and Distribution of Coral Reefs,* made it plain that reef corals grow most vigorously in water less than 90 feet deep and that they are unable to live at all below about 150 feet.

Clearly, no particular problem arises in explaining the development of fringing reefs since these are always close to land, which acts as a suitable platform for the commencement of coral growth. To account for barrier reefs, up to 100 miles from land, or for atolls, sometimes thousands of miles from land and surrounded by very deep water, the earlier naturalists assumed that ring-shaped atolls grew from the edges of extinct volcanoes lying close beneath the surface of the ocean. This, however, does not explain the barrier reefs.

Darwin produced, as a result of careful study, a theory which fits all the known facts to a remarkable degree and accounts for the presence not only of atolls but also of barrier reefs. This theory is mainly still held today, but a number of later writers have added to it on the basis of more recent information. According to Darwin, all coral reefs then known were situated in areas where, at some time in the past, a sinking of the earth had taken place. This subsidence theory explains the formation of both atolls and barrier reefs with admirable simplicity.

The first stage of the formation of an atoll or a barrier reef was thought by Darwin to be a fringing reef (Fig. 7). A reef of this type might be expected to grow on the shore of any continent or island in tropical seas where other conditions were suitable. As the land began slowly to subside, the reef would continue to grow upward and outward. So, unless the subsidence were too rapid, coral growth could keep pace with it. The continued sinking of the land would increase the distance between the reef and the shore so that a deep, wide channel would develop, and the reef would now have all the characteristics of a barrier reef. If the land happened to be a small island, it would eventually disappear below the surface and

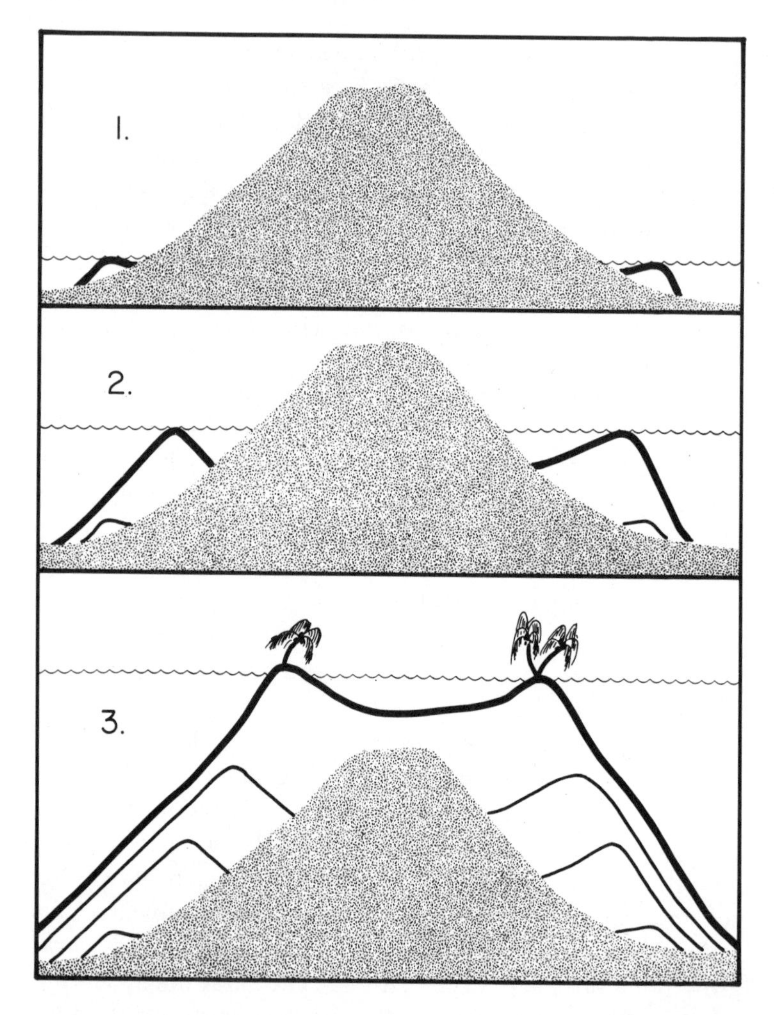

Figure 7. Sections illustrating the formation of barrier reefs and atolls according to Darwin's theory. 1, 2, and 3 are the successive stages in the sinking of land beneath the water. 1. Fringing reef; 2. Barrier; and 3. Atoll. Simplified and not to scale. The palm trees are grossly exaggerated and serve to indicate islets.

the barrier reef would now be an atoll, by continuation of its upward growth.

Geologic evidence to support this theory was discovered by the American scientist J. D. Dana in the general appearance and topography of many of the islands with barrier reefs. Others, however, found gaps in the Darwinian theory, and rival theories were advanced. None of these has supplanted that of Darwin, but each has added something to the general understanding of reef formation.

One of the two principal objections to the universal application of the subsidence theory was based on the fact that fringing reefs often exist in the same general area as barrier reefs. Since Darwin's theory requires that fringing reefs continue existence only on a stationary coast and barrier reefs form only on a subsiding coast, the areas in question would of necessity be in the paradoxical situation of both sinking and remaining stationary. This objection, however, has been partially answered by the more recent observations of W. M. Davis and of his predecessors, who suggest that a tilting of the continental margin might occur, thus causing a sinking in one place and rising in another close by.

The subsidence theory would lead one to expect that atolls should have lagoons considerably deeper than 180 feet, the maximum actually observed. Furthermore, the widespread and prolonged sinking of the earth's surface in all the coral seas simultaneously, which Darwin's theory demanded, was considered by many to be highly improbable. These and other objections finally led to the theory advanced by Sir John Murray, one of the great scientists who took part in the celebrated four-year expedition of H.M.S. *Challenger,* between 1872 and 1876.

Murray concluded that the platforms upon which reefs

are built originate as submarine ridges, probably of volcanic origin. These would not necessarily come close enough to the surface for corals to begin their growth, but they would become shallower with time as the result of an accumulation of fine limestone silt formed by skeletons of foraminifera and other microscopic animals, which are always present in the ocean in countless millions and which are continually falling to the bottom. It was well known, in fact, that large areas of chalky rock now part of land were originally formed by similar deposits on the ocean floor. Since coral grows more rapidly on the outside of a reef and tends to die as a result of sediment in the more sheltered inner portions, the innumerable ring-shaped atolls would be explained without widespread sinking of the earth's crust.

Further suggestions include the theory that non-reef building corals, which are able to live in deep water, were responsible for building up the platforms. Other theories are based upon the belief that islands might be cut down by wave action and water currents to form the base upon which the reefs have grown.

An important contribution to the subject was the glacial control theory advanced by R. A. Daly. According to Daly, all existent coral reefs have been formed since the last glacial epoch. During the periods of glaciation, the continents at high latitude were covered by ice caps several thousand feet thick and extending considerably below the polar circles into what are now the temperate latitudes. The result of trapping such great quantities of water on the continents was a general lowering of sea level by about 175 feet so that all previously formed coral reefs were killed by exposure to air. The former ocean bottom, exposed by the withdrawal of water and no longer protected by reefs, was cut back by wave action so that broad platforms were penetrating the limestone caps of these atolls to their supposed volcanic basements, as postulated earlier by Sir John Murray. This was finally accomplished in 1951 when two holes were drilled on Eniwetok Atoll to depths of 4222 feet and 4610 feet. Following this, two more drillings were made on Midway Atoll in the northern Marshall Islands. Both holes reached volcanic basement at depths of 1261 and 1270 feet. Additional data were also gathered by dredging samples from the outer slopes of various atolls and comparing this material with that of the core drillings from corresponding depths.

These achievements and the discovery by H. H. Hess in 1946 of about 160 submerged flat-topped sea mounts, or guyots as he termed them, between the Marianas and the Hawaiian Islands have provided a much better base for evaluating theories of the origin of coral atolls. In the northern Marshall Islands guyots are distributed along the same chain as atolls, their upper surfaces ranging between 3000 to 6000 feet below the present sea level. As they have some features in common with atolls, it is possible that some genetic relationship exists. Guyots are generally similar to atolls in size and shape. However, several points of difference exist.

(1) Volcanic rocks have been dredged up from the top of guyots but only on the lower flanks of atolls, the latter being covered by coral growth on the upper portion.

(2) The side slopes of the upper 500 fathoms of atolls are about twice as steep as those of the upper 500 fathoms of the guyots.

(3) The periphery of the guyot is rounded in profile in contrast to the sharp reef edge of the atolls.

(4) The highest point on a guyot is at the center while on an atoll it is at the edges.

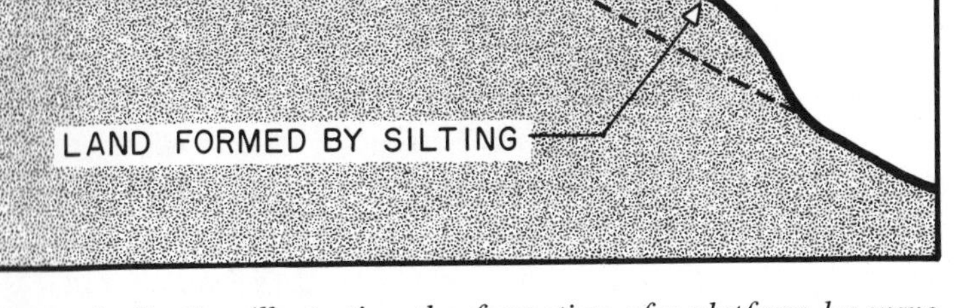

Figure 8. Section illustrating the formation of a platform by wave action in the marginal seas during glaciation.

formed around the land (Fig. 8). When an ice age passed, the sea level rose to its normal position and engulfed the platforms. As it became warmer, the modern reefs began to grow upon these new bases, which were all at a depth of less than 175 feet and therefore suitable for coral growth.

In general it may be said that Darwin's subsidence theory combined with Daly's glacial control theory is adequate to explain most known reefs; but there are also undoubted cases where the platforms have been formed by agencies of a different nature. During the celebrated expeditions to Funafuti Atoll, to the north of the Fiji Islands, a bore-hole was drilled to a depth of over 1000 feet. According to Darwinian theory, it might be expected that the core from such a boring would consist of dead coral entirely, formed by upward growth as the underlying land mass continued to sink (Fig. 9). The theories of submarine ridges and accumulated sediments would, on the contrary, lead one to expect a core of silt at a depth of less than 175 feet, with the ancient rocks of the submarine ridge below. When the actual core was examined, it was found to consist of coral fragments only, thus supporting Darwin's theory. Objections were raised, however, on the grounds that the bore might have traversed the outer edge or talus slope of the atoll, and so missed the sedimentary and volcanic rocks.

Although the question was left open, much was learned about atolls prior to 1946. In addition to the previously mentioned Funafuti expedition, the Japanese, between 1934 and 1936, drilled a hole on the reefs of the small island of Kita-Daito (North Borodino) to a depth of 1416 feet (Ladd and Tracey, 1949). This then represented man's understanding of coral reef formation up until the year 1946.

With the advent of World War II and man's newfound ability to release large quantities of energy through nuclear fission, isolated proving grounds were required. In order to gain a maximum of technical information from these weapon tests, a thorough understanding of the physical and biological environment of the proving grounds was necessary. To this end, in 1947 American scientists drilled six holes on Bikini Atoll. Two of these were very deep, 1346 and 2556 feet, respectively, and the others only 100 to 300 feet deep. These drillings were described in detail by Emery, Tracey, and Ladd (1949). A drilling in Maratoea reef limestone to a depth of over 1300 feet was reported by Kuenen (1947). This, however, was not an atoll, and Maratoea does not have a volcanic base.

None of the holes mentioned thus far succeeded in

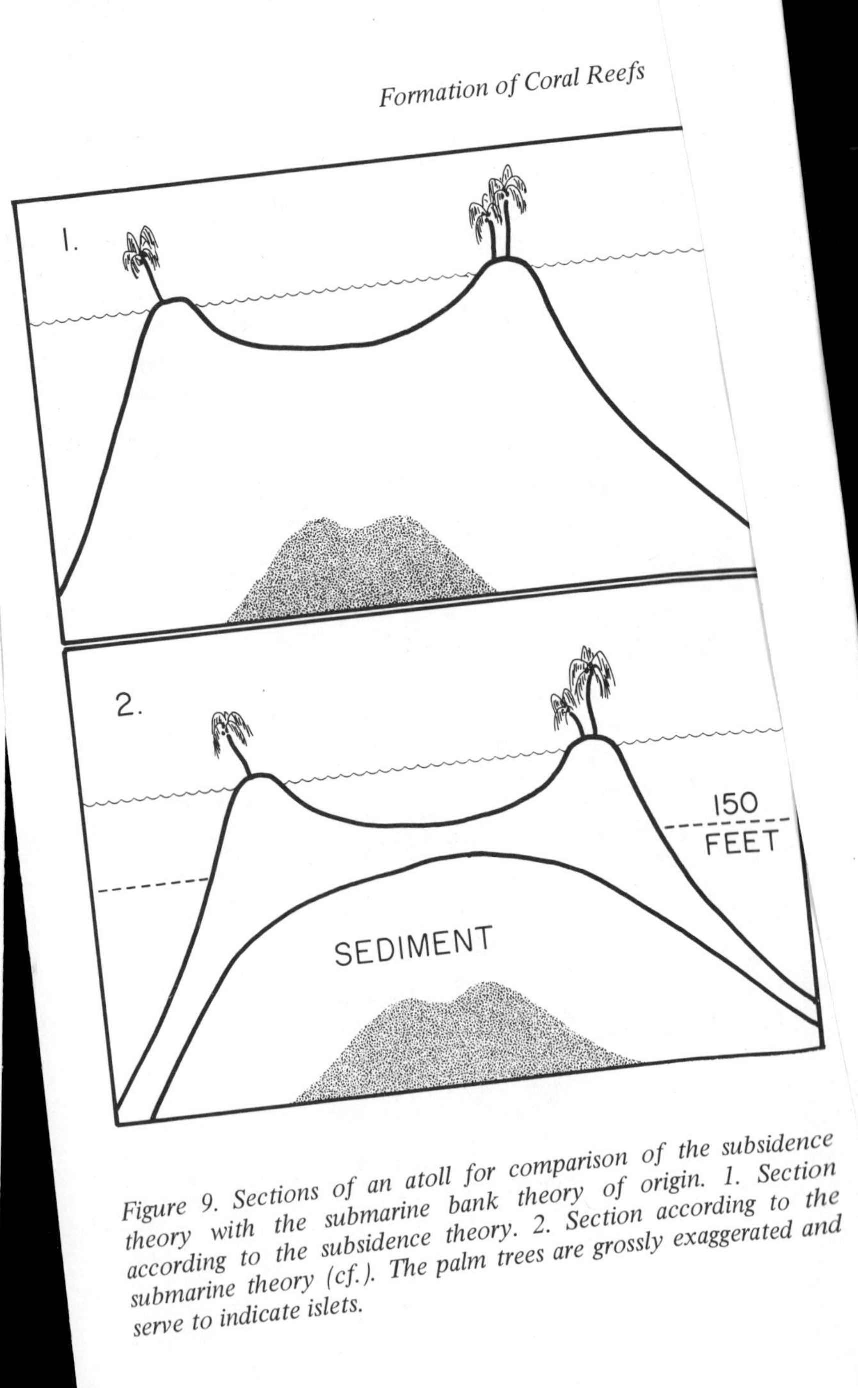

Figure 9. Sections of an atoll for comparison of the subsidence theory with the submarine bank theory of origin. 1. Section according to the subsidence theory. 2. Section according to the submarine theory (cf.). The palm trees are grossly exaggerated and serve to indicate islets.

(5) The presence of volcanic rocks on guyots suggests that they are fault blocks, unmodified volcanoes, or volcanoes beveled by past wave action.

Seismic refraction work done by the 1950 mid-Pacific expedition under the leadership of Russell Raitt provided a clearer picture of the structural relationship between guyots and atolls. A profile of the volcanic rock foundation of Bikini Atoll and its relationship to nearby Sylvania Guyot showed that the volcanic rock that formed the guyot continued under the atoll, rising well above the guyot as an irregular surface (Emery, Tracey, and Ladd, 1954). This indicates that guyots and atolls are fundamentally alike. It also suggests that atoll foundations are never completely beveled by wave action and that they thus project into the zone of reef growth and become reef crowned, whereas guyots remained without such a cap. To explain the absence of coral structures on guyots, Hess (1948) suggested that guyots were formed during the Pre-Cambrian era, more than 600 million years ago and prior to the evolution of corals, whereas atolls could be much younger features, as their reef caps would suggest.

From the standpoint of the origin of atolls, the great thickness of reef limestones discovered by drilling the atolls of Funafuti, Bikini, Eniwetok, and Midway suggests that the reefs were built up from submerging or subsiding foundations that have sunk several thousands of feet since the reefs began. Glacial control was important during the past million years, for it is now known that sea level has changed as much as 350 feet between glacial and interglacial ages.

Cesare Emiliani (1966), using oxygen isotope techniques, has determined the following temperature variations of the surface ocean water during the Pleistocene epoch:

Region	Glacial	Interglacial
Caribbean	20° C	27° C
Equatorial Atlantic	20° C	26° C
Equatorial Pacific	21° C	25° C

Knowing the temperature requirements of living corals, it is evident that coral growth could have been inhibited during the glacial ages.

All the volcanoes of the Pacific below existing atolls were at least partially leveled by wave action during the later part of the Mesozoic era, some 80 million years ago. Owing to differences in size or density or to some other cause, such as local changes in the earth's structure or tectonic activity, they sank at different rates. Those that sank slowly or were incompletely beveled were the sites of vigorous coral growth that maintained their upper surfaces in shallow water. Those that became completely beveled and had sinking rates in excess of the coral growth rate formed those structures known as flat-topped sea mounts or guyots. Thus, almost 100 years later, most students of coral reef formation still accept the ingenious theory developed by Charles Darwin during the famous voyage of H.M.S. *Beagle* in 1836.

Those who would care to know more of the mechanisms of coral reef origin and the facts upon which the theories are based should consult *The Coral Reef Problem* by W. M. Davis and *Atoll Environment and Ecology* by Harold J. Wiens. These provide the best and most exhaustive of modern accounts. They are of a technical nature, however, written from the geologist's viewpoint. The general reader may prefer the first chapter of C. M. Yonge's book, *A Year on the Great Barrier Reef,* which contains an excellent account of the general subject as well as a detailed description of the Great Barrier Reef, written in nontechnical language.

3

Western Atlantic Reefs

THE WESTERN Atlantic coral reefs, formed under different conditions than those of the reefs previously discussed, lie within what Davis (1928) has called the marginal belt. This is an area between lower and higher latitudes that was greatly affected by the glacial ages. Whereas the low latitudes did not become too cold for the continued life and growth of corals, reef corals in the marginal areas died during glaciation. As a result, the shore remained unprotected and waves wore away the coast and formed a platform around it, just below sea level. Debris from the wearing away of the land added offshore material to the platform (Fig. 8).

Toward the end of each glacial age, when the seas became warmer, reef corals were again able to live in marginal areas. Reefs were formed upon the platforms. These, now called bank reefs, are characterized by being farther from shore than a fringing reef but having a shallower lagoon channel than a barrier reef. Moreover, they are often at some distance inside the seaward edge of the platform and do not grow at the edge of deep water as do true atolls and barriers.

Bank reefs range from the Parcel das Paredes reefs of middle Brazil, by way of Cape San Roque to the north, along the Lesser Antilles and, finally, to the Florida Keys and Bermuda. Often, reefs living in the warm seas of Tertiary times, as long as 50 million years ago, formed a great part of the platforms upon which the present day reefs are growing.

A description of the different coral reef areas of the western Atlantic will show various modifications of the marginal belt processes outlined above.

Bermuda has a most interesting history. During the geologic epoch known as the Eocene, between 40 and 50 million years ago, it was a volcano that later subsided below the surface of the ocean and was worn down by wave action. In the later Tertiary period it sank further while being covered with marine limestones. There is some evidence that an atoll grew on the bank during this period. However, later on, the coral mass was once more exposed and formed an island of about 230 square miles (Davis, 1928; Sayles, 1931). This exposure was due to the drop in sea level resulting from glaciation. During this exposure, submarine accumulation of debris resulting from wave action formed a shallow-water platform surrounding the exposed land. Finally, rising and warmer sea allowed the present reefs to grow. They are comparatively weak and able to exist only by virtue of the warm Gulf Stream water.

Florida possesses bank reefs which, like those of Bermuda, rarely reach the surface. They are built upon a broad, shallow platform which was once the bottom of a shallow sea covering the southern portion of the south-eastern United States. The platform was then raised above the surface and worn by wind and rain. The eroded land surface was eventually submerged again and remained so during the Tertiary period. During this time, a number of reefs were formed over a considerable part of the area. Much later, within the last million years, the land was periodically exposed and flooded as a result of the withdrawal of water during glacial ages and its release during interglacial times. The Pleistocene reefs which grew during these changes formed rock 100 feet thick. At the time of the last glacial age, while the sea level was low, a platform was cut into the land. As the ice caps melted for the last time, the platform was once again flooded. Today it forms the base for the coral reefs growing off the Florida Keys. As a result of independent earth movements, however, a portion of the Pleistocene reefs, 120,000 years old, still remains above water to form the line of keys extending from Miami to Key West and the Dry Tortugas.

The living reefs are situated a mile or two offshore from the Keys. Between the reefs and the Keys a process of chemical and mechanical sedimentation is slowly filling in the channel, where small patches of reef heads exist. The reefs do not extend north of Fowey Rocks for two reasons: the drop in temperature as one travels north, and a southward drift of siliceous sands which kill or restrict coral growth by silting action.

At the southwestern extremity of the Keys are the Marquesas and Tortugas reefs. They are ring-shaped reefs built on the shallow sediment banks, which have been improperly called atolls. They are not associated directly with subsidence, nor are they fringed by deep water in the way true atolls are. While the shallow muddy bottoms west of Florida do not offer a sound foothold for corals, biologists of the School of Marine and Atmospheric Science of the University of Miami have recently found reef coral growth in depths of 50 to 150 feet off Tarpon Springs.

The Florida reefs are best studied some miles south of Miami and are easily examined with a glass face mask while diving off a small boat. Many of the smaller coral species may be found closer inshore by those willing to wade a short distance off the Florida Keys. Some are found as far north as the shores of Elliot Key or on the bars south of Biscayne Key. In small patches, reef corals are found considerably north of Miami, but only offshore and in relatively deep water.

The reefs of the Bahamas were formed by the same general processes that produced those off Florida. The living reefs, however, are much better developed, and those to the east of the islands of Abaco, Eleuthera, and Andros are very extensive. The reefs that protect the northern shore of New Providence, to the east and west of Nassau, are particularly well situated for observation by the visitor.

Much of the present land of the Bahamas was accumulated as chemical deposits in the lagoons of preglacial atolls. The platforms on which the present reefs stand were formed during a glacial period when the sea was over 250 feet below its present level. In some respects reef types in areas near Cuba and Jamaica are closer to the types found in the Pacific. There are several true atolls, notably Hogsty Reef, to the east of Cuba, and the drowned atoll of Cay Sal Bank, between Cuba and the Florida Keys.

Off the north coast of Cuba are the Colorados barrier reefs. They lie up to 20 miles offshore and extend from

Cape San Antonio to Bahia Honda. Other reefs on the north coast extend from east of Havana to Nuevitas Bay. There are scattered reefs only at the eastern end of the island. The southern reef is similar to the Florida reefs. It grows at some distance back from the edge of the shelf and is not a barrier reef of the true coral seas type. This formation is best developed east and west of the Isle of Pines, where it guards the Gulf of Batabano, and also between Trinidad and Cape Cruz. Together, these are the longest reefs in the West Indies.

The West Indies generally conform to the foregoing descriptions with some variation in detail. The reef structure of Barbados consists of a series of fringing reefs formed during uplift (Mesolella et al., 1969). These old reefs form terraces dating from 80,000 to more than 200,000 years ago.

Reef formations are present to a limited extent off the Gulf coast of Mexico on the Campeche Bank, where they form the Alacran Reef, and near Veracruz. Apart from these, the Gulf of Mexico has no significant reef formations.

The British Honduras reefs are well developed. They extend almost continuously for over 125 miles, which is the longest unbroken formation in the West Indies. Both bank and barrier reefs are found here.

An imperfect atoll occurs at Los Roques, 70 miles north of the coast of Venezuela. The Lesser Antilles all possess living reefs of the marginal sea type that grew upon platforms formed by the abrasion of wave action during interglacial ages.

The Jamaican reefs have been studied in greater detail than others, especially by T. F. Goreau. They are fringing reefs that have developed on a narrow offshore shelf, less than 1500 feet wide, probably within the past 5000 years. A peculiarity of these reefs is that, at a depth of about 25 fathoms, they become very steep fronted, unlike the bank reefs, which usually grow at some distance inshore from the bank edge.

4

Structure and Habits of Living Corals

THE BEAUTIFUL white stony corals which are sold for ornaments in curio shops bear little resemblance to the living green, gold, or orange corals. In fact, they are merely the bleached skeletons of their former selves. The creature which forms the skeleton is an animal very low in the scale of evolution and is very similar in general structure to a sea anemone. A sea anemone grows attached to rocks and consists essentially of a soft, tubular body with a mouth opening at one end, surrounded by a ring of hollow tentacles. Within the mouth opening, the skin projects inward to form a passage, or throat, known as the stomodoeum.

In its simplest form the coral is the skeleton of a simple anemone-like creature known as a polyp (see Fig. 10). The outer layer of the skin covering the lower part of the polyp has the peculiar capacity of forming on its surface a stony calcium carbonate layer, much as the skin of an oyster forms a shell. Since the polyp is tubular, the stony layer takes the shape of a limestone cup. In many corals, a short, pillar-like infold of skin in the center of the base forms a vertical axial rod called the columella.

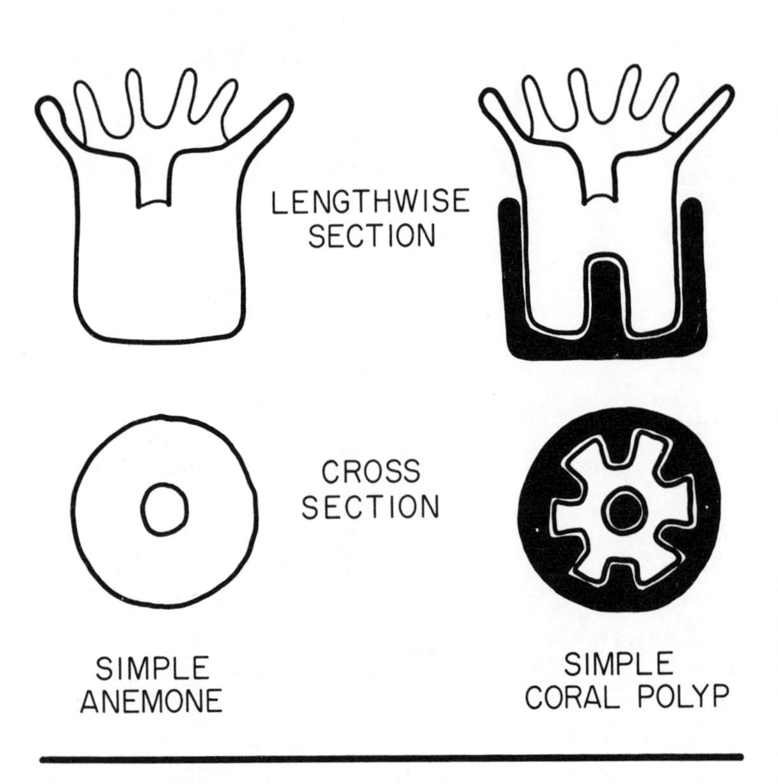

Figure 10. Lengthwise and cross sections of a simple anemone and a simple coral. The mesenteric folds of the body wall which project into the interior are omitted for the sake of clarity. Dark portion represents stony skeleton.

The coral polyp is complicated by vertical folds of the wall of the tube. There are two types of folds, one of which consists of an infolding of the entire body wall. These folds project radially toward the interior of the cylindrical polyp. The skin turned inside by the folds was originally part of the outside of the polyp and it continues to deposit calcium carbonate. In this way it forms radial stony partitions called septa, projecting from the wall of the coral cup inward toward the columella. In some corals there is little development beyond this stage, and the polyp merely forms a single cup with radiating plates inside it. Most corals, however, develop by growth in size and complexity of the individual polyp, or by branching and multiplication of polyps. The polyp may enlarge and grow out sideways into lobes, without dividing or branching, so that it eventually becomes flower-shaped. Since the coral cup grows with the polyp, it too will become flower-shaped (Plate 26), or, where considerable outgrowth takes place, it may eventually become convoluted as in the brain corals (Plate 19). In most corals, as the individual polyp continues to grow, its cup becomes longer and more tubular. At the same time, the polyp branches to form daughter polyps and the original cup now becomes two. As the process continues, the older part of the tube is cut off by transverse partitions and a chambered mass of limestone rock is developed (Fig. 11). When the polyps are only loosely connected, a branched structure results (Plates 28, 48).

In other cases the polyps may remain close together and the cups become united into a compact mass (Fig. 11 and Plate 31). Sometimes the coral mass itself is branched, with small cups projecting over the entire surface as they bud off from the main polyp (Plate 3). Thus, in various ways, the small anemone-like polyp eventually forms large masses of rock of considerable weight, with the overall production running possibly into billions of tons each year. The stony rocks developed by the polyps vary greatly in appearance from small, delicate

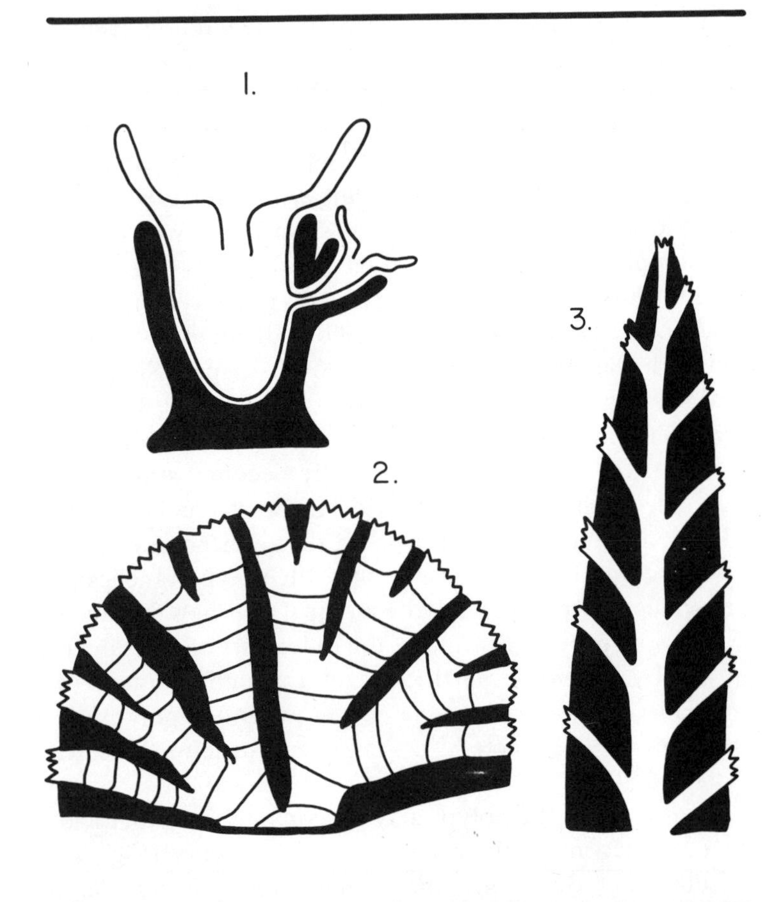

Figure 11. Lengthwise sections of corals illustrating modes of branching and colony formation. Greatly simplified. 1. Lateral budding of a single polyp. 2. Formation of a massive colony by growth and branching of the polyps, showing transverse partitions laid down as growth of the polyp progresses. 3. Growth in which the original polyp continues to remain at the apex, forming branching colonies similar to Acropora. Dark portion represents stony skeleton.

cups to tree-like branching colonies or enormous boulders.

In addition to the folds of skin which form the septa or radial plates, the coral polyp possesses a second type of internal fold. This second type, known as a mesentery, is an infolding of the inner lining only. For the sake of simplicity, mesenteries have been omitted from the previous diagrams. During the breeding season, eggs and spermatozoa begin to develop in the swollen edges of the mesentery. When they are ripe, the spermatozoa of one polyp are released through the mouth and are carried by water currents until they eventually reach another polyp. Here they are drawn into the mouth by the water currents that are set up to bring food into the coral animal. In this manner they reach the inside of another polyp and fertilize the eggs while they are still attached to the mesentery. After a short period of development, the eggs are set free and leave through the mouth of the parent. At this stage they are in the form of small pear-shaped bodies about the size of a pinhead. Small, rapidly beating hairs or cilia clothe the surface of the coral larvae and give them a limited swimming ability. The stage at which the larva is drifting or swimming feebly in the water may last from one to three weeks, but settling on suitable substrate probably occurs within a few days. During the swimming period, the larva may be carried a considerable distance by ocean currents and wind drifts, thus accounting for the presence of living corals on such isolated reefs as those of Bermuda and many of the lonely Pacific islands. The shortness of the free-swimming planula stage in some species, however, may also account for absence of corals in some regions where the environment may be otherwise suitable. If the larva reaches a suitably hard surface, it attaches by means of a cementing substance formed at one end and grows into a small tube. The upper end is indented to form a fleshy cup which later becomes the mouth. Tentacles grow out from the rim of the upper surface and the skin immediately begins to form the stony skeleton of the first polyp of a new colony.

The tentacles are withdrawn during the daytime, but at night they are expanded for the purpose of catching food. This is thought to consist of small animals, principally crustacea, although some of the larger polyps such as *Manicina areolata* have been observed to eat very small fish. Each tentacle possesses large numbers of stinging cells, or nematocysts. These are able to shoot out microscopic poison darts which paralyze the prey. The tentacles then turn toward the mouth, and the food is passed inside. In some cases feeding is helped by the beating of small hairs or cilia that cover the upper surface of the polyp. The food is rapidly digested by juices formed by the mesenteries.

All reef-building corals contain within their tissues a large number of very small, single-celled plants known as zooxanthellae (blue-green algae). Since plants take in carbon dioxide from their surroundings and give off oxygen, the coral benefits from their presence by obtaining a supply of oxygen in its tissues for breathing. In the same manner the algae are able to use the carbon dioxide which is given off continually in the breathing of all animal tissues. The waste products of the coral are also useful to the algae and perhaps vice versa. Thus the strange association of a plant living inside an animal is mutually beneficial.

The rate at which corals grow has been the subject of a considerable amount of experimentation. Results obtained in a number of studies by T. W. Vaughan, J. E. Hoffmeister, and by Shinn, show that on the Florida and

Bahamas reefs the increase in diameter varies from about 1/2 to nearly 2 inches per year. In 23 years a brain coral measured in the Pacific by Dr. Mayor had grown from 30 to 76 inches. It is easy to appreciate, in the light of these figures, that corals may, over a period of years, grow into dangerous obstructions to navigation in channels once considered safe, and they have built up considerable masses of land during the long period of geological history.

5

Associates of Living Corals

CORALS are not the only reef builders or inhabitants of coral reefs. An amazing variety of other living creatures is associated with them, some building up the limestone formation and others actively tearing it down.

Living in the coral rock itself are various burrowing or boring animals, which riddle it with holes and passages so that the rock breaks apart. Certain encrusting sponges, yellow, lavender, purple, or red in color, are found on the surface of the rock or of sea shells; one of these, *Cliona,* eats its way into the rock by means of a dissolution process. Other sponges of various shapes and colors are attached to the surface of coral rock. Certain strange worm-like creatures, the gephyrids, form burrows and are seen only when the coral is broken apart. The spiny sea urchins or sea eggs, spherical or ovoid in shape and covered with spines, possess chisel-like teeth that enable them to eat pockets into the rock. Among these is the long, black-spined sea urchin, *Centrechinus antillarum.* A smaller species, more ovoid in shape with shorter purple spines, is *Echinometra lucunter.* Still another sea urchin, *Eucidaris tribuloides,* has fewer spines which are short and thick so that it is appropriately called the club-spined urchin.

Some of the sea shells, including *Pholas, Gastrochaena*, and *Lithophaga,* have adopted a burrowing form of life. Associated with the coral by attachment, but not forming extensive burrows, are numerous other shells such as the wing shells, *Pteria* and *Pinctada*; the ark shells, *Arca* and *Barbatia*; the date mussel, *Modiolus*; and the scallop shells, *Pecten* and *Lima.* The jewel box shell, *Chama,* and the so-called reef oyster, *Spondylus,* are well known to collectors. The strange oyster *Ostrea frons*, with hook-like outgrowths from the shell whereby it attaches itself, is often found on corals or seafans. Two genera of pelecypods, *Lima* and *Pteria*, are found trapped alive in the rock by the growth of the living coral around them.

Sea worms similar to those commonly used for bait are able to bore through the living rock with their powerful jaws. One of these, *Eunice furcata,* has the peculiar habit of breaking off the hindmost part of the body. This portion, which contains the eggs, then leaves the burrow and swims to the surface of the water, after which the eggs are released by breakdown of the body enclosing them. This happens at a certain phase of the moon during the early morning in midsummer—the careful observer may see the surface of the ocean above the reef literally alive with wriggling worms. In the Pacific islands where a similar phenomenon takes place, the so-called Palolo worms are highly esteemed as food. Some worms do not destroy the rock but line their burrows with a porcelain-like material for protection. The head of the living worm, which projects into the surrounding water, looks like a beautifully colored flower. A slight movment or shadow, however, will cause retraction into the burrow so quickly that the withdrawal is almost undetectable.

Sea anemones and seasquirts are frequently associated with corals—the rock is often encrusted with brightly colored growths of seamats or Bryozoa. Certain barnacles, *Creusia* and *Pyrgoma,* become attached, and as the coral grows around them they may become entrapped so that they appear as gall-like swellings on the rock surface, each with a small slit through which the appendages of the barnacle project in search of food. In a somewhat similar manner the gall crabs *Hapalocarcinus* and *Cryptochirus* become entombed in the living coral.

"Stinging coral" is superficially similar to true coral but is not closely related. It grows into small branches like miniature staghorns or forms encrustations on the surface of old coral or dead seawhips. The polyps are very small, so the skeleton is easily distinguished from true coral by the lack of visible cups. Instead, the surface is covered by fine, barely visible holes, accounting for the scientific name, *Millepora.* The stinging cells of this false coral are sufficiently powerful to develop an irritating rash when handled with bare fingers.

A distinct contribution to the material of reef limestone is made by the so-called soft corals, often referred to as seafans and seawhips. These brightly colored organisms are related to corals, although they differ in many respects. The common seawhips, known as *Pseudopterogorgia acerosa,* consist of long whip-like branches, the surfaces of which are covered with small, barely visible polyps. The axis of each branch is a horny skeleton. Embedded in the flesh surrounding the skeleton are numerous, small limestone spicules, which add to the coral sand when the whip dies. Much thicker and heavier than the seawhip, forming finger-like branches or even thick encrustations, is the beautiful purple *Briareum asbestinum.* The numerous fair-sized polyps form a thick fur on the living seafinger.

Seafans, as their name indicates, grow in the shape of large blue, purple, or yellow leaf-like expanses. Their basic structure is similar to that of seawhips, but the numerous short branches are interlaced and fused together to form a close network. The common seafan in the West Indies is *Gorgonia flabellum.*

A varied collection of Crustacea is found in the crevices among hard corals, around the bases of soft corals, and in the burrows formed by other animals. The small, bright green stomatopod *Gonodactylus* is frequently seen here. There are also snapping shrimps; little more than an inch or so long, they are capable of making very loud clicking noises as they snap shut the giant claws that are asymmetrically developed on the leg of one side. The female of this crustacean may be carrying bright orange egg masses. In addition there are masked crabs with their bodies camouflaged by algae, hydroids, or other small sea growths that are attached to their backs. In the open or in the larger crevices are spider crabs, large mantis shrimps (*Squilla empusa*), the edible spiny lobster or crayfish (*Panulirus argus*), and many species of larger crabs. In the crevices between the rocks or in burrows in the sand are occasionally found the edible stone crab, *Menippe,* or the weird looking, shovel-nosed, Spanish lobster, *Scyllarides equinoctialis.* Occasionally an octopus may also be encountered.

Less closely associated with the corals are the enormous loggerhead sponges *Spheciospongia vesparia*, the large cup sponge—sometimes larger than a small barrel—and the black commercial wool, reef, and grass sponges. Other brilliantly colored sponges, tubular, spherical, encrusting, or branching, grow on the bottom. The microscopic silica spicules contained in the tissues of many of these sponges are released at death and contribute to the unconsolidated sediments in and around the reef tract.

Living independently of the coral are also the small, red starfish *Echinaster sentus,* the six armed starfish *Linckia guildingii,* and the giant starfish *Oreaster reticulata.* These possess limestone skeletons consisting of ossicles. The dark colored, leathery skinned sea cucumber, *Holothuria floridana,* moves like a giant slug over the bottom and extracts nutrient by forcing the sand through its body. If interfered with, it may eject its entire set of internal organs and crawl away to grow them anew. Some of its relatives have very delicate transparent skin and may live in the interstices of the rocks. *Euapta lappa,* one of these, may be crammed full of coarse sand, yet it is so delicate that it falls apart on handling.

Close relatives of the sea urchins are the potato urchins, *Clypeaster rosaceus,* which live among weeds or burrow in the sand. Greatly flattened versions of these are the sand dollars, which are also found in the sand between masses of coral.

Many of the coral reef animals that are not closely associated with the coral itself live among the so-called sea grasses which grow in the quieter, shallower waters behind the outer reef. These grasses are not seaweeds but are really flowering plants which have become adapted to life under the ocean. The most common is the flat-bladed turtle grass, *Thallassia.*

Certain marine algae and seaweeds living on the reef and in the shallow lagoons deposit limestone in their living tissues, and so they also add to the sand and rock of coral reefs. A common alga is *Halimeda,* bright green in color with branches that have the appearance of flat, triangular beads strung together. Sometimes it occurs in very large clumps, particularly in shallow water near the shore. Other kinds of limestone seaweeds are coralline algae known as nullipores that form heavy encrustations and, in the Pacific at least, are an important factor in building up the reef. On the western Atlantic reefs these coralline algae are much less conspicuous, although a common form of calcareous algae in this region is *Lithothamnion,* which grows in delicate branching form in various colors.

The species of conchs, whelks, cowries, cone shells, olive shells, tulip shells, limpets, and other seasnails which inhabit the reef are so numerous that their discussion would require an entire book. The same is true of the bivalve shells such as the oysters and their relatives, the scallop shells, clams, wing shells, chamas, cockles, and mussels. Although space does not permit a description of these, the bibliography contains selected references to handbooks specially written for their identification.

Fishes associated with the coral reefs are so numerous that they are numbered by the hundreds of species and may only be briefly mentioned here. A common characteristic of those which make their homes among the coral boulders is the amazing brilliance of color and design. Foremost in point of brilliance of color are the angel fish, queen trigger fish, demoiselles, and parrot fish. Groupers and giant jewfish live among the rocks, where the vicious moray eel also waits for its prey. Sharks and barracudas are always found, although the reef is just one of the places where they search for food.

Among the larger associates of coral reefs are the loggerhead, hawksbill, and green turtles, which move to the sandy beaches to lay their eggs. Between the reef and the land, on grassy or sandy bottoms, the sting rays and leopard rays are common and, much more rarely, the giant manta ray or devilfish is seen.

Thus, not only the coral, but a complex community of animals living together comprises the living reef. Some break down the rock and some build it up, but all contribute in some form or other to the rock, sand, mud, and detritus. Crevices between the smaller particles are filled with dead limestone skeletons of the microscopic foraminifera, coccoliths, and other tiny creatures which drift suspended in the seawater during their short lives and which add to the bottom deposits when they die. Lime may be dissolved from the rock and sand and become redeposited as a cement. This is the manner in which the smaller grains and larger boulders were fused together to form the solid coral rock that is underlying the soil of the Florida Keys and certain other parts of the Atlantic coral area now exposed by a lower sea level.

6

Collection and Preparation of Corals

WHEREAS the collection of coral specimens from the outer reef involves the use of a boat and necessitates diving, a great number of coral species may be collected by simply wading in shallow water in appropriate localities. A glass-bottomed bucket is useful in finding specimens, particularly when the wind makes the water choppy. Most of the corals found in shallow water are loose or only lightly attached to the underlying rock. The larger reef corals are firmly cemented to the bottom and a tire iron or crowbar is required to break them off, or to pry loose portions small enough to handle. Some of these are found in very shallow water but the majority occur in the deeper water of the outer reef. While some of them, particularly the branching forms, may be broken loose with a strong, multiple-pronged grapnel, the most satisfactory method is to dive to the bottom and collect the specimens by hand. This can be accomplished by a good swimmer using conventional face mask, snorkel, and flippers.

From what has been said in Chapter 1, it will be realized that corals are sensitive to their surroundings. Some species are more sensitive than others and are virtually restricted to a specific environment. Others, more hardy, are found over a wider environmental range.

Even in a single species, moreover, the form and appearance of the coral may vary greatly depending upon the nature of the surroundings. In rough water there is a tendency toward more massive or encrusting growth or (in branching forms) to the development of short, thick branches. Where the water is quieter, diffuse branching or thin projecting plates occur. In deeper water, below the region of greatest wave action, the spindle-shaped or pillar-like form is evident.

For example, the finger coral, *Porites porites,* is more openly branched with more slender branches in shallow, relatively quiet water. On the reef itself, where wave action is more vigorous, the same species is compactly branched and each finger is short, thick, and stubby. The brain coral, *Diploria clivosa,* forms a low encrusting growth in regions of heavy surge, but in deeper water, where it is less exposed to wave movement, it tends to become more massive and to develop knobs and blunt projections.

Species found in the region of heaviest wave action on the exposed reef are usually the massive or boulder types such as *Montastrea annularis,* the brain corals, the porous coral *Porites astreoides,* and the starlet coral *Siderastrea siderea.* There are also thick branching forms like the elkhorn coral, *Acropora palmata,* and, in the outermost part of the reef, the thick columns of *Dendrogyra cylindrus,* the pillar coral. There are no fragile branches or unattached species.

At the opposite extreme of living conditions, in shallow water where sediment is present, are found the finger coral, *Porites furcata,* and also the more slender form of

Porites porites, the clubbed finger coral. Small, rounded masses of *Siderastrea radians* are also found here, along with the common rose coral, *Manicina areolata.* These, together with *Favia fragum,* are most resistant to the effects of sediment, fluctuating temperature, and exposure to the atmosphere during very low tides.

Some of the shallow-water corals may be found in deeper water, but few of the deeper water corals are able to live in shallow water. In the intermediate depths there is a good deal of intermingling.

A curious effect of sediment is often seen in the fairly deep water behind the reef, where some of the massive corals are able to live but where sediment is nevertheless present and tends to settle on the upper surface of the coral boulder. The uppermost horizontal part of the surface is killed by the fine particles that settle on it, but the outer, more steeply sloping sides continue to grow so that the coral assumes a doughnut shape.

Having collected the coral specimen, one may preserve it several ways. The color of the living colony cannot be retained by any practical method, but the general appearance of the live coral is kept by preserving it in industrial ethyl alcohol of about 70% strength. If immediately placed in this, the polyps will contract, but they may be killed in an expanded condition if kept awhile in a dish of seawater in the dark. When they are fully expanded, a cotton bag containing magnesium sulphate is immersed in the water. The slowly dissolving crystals narcotize the polyps so that after a while they do not contract even when placed in the alcohol preservative.

As a rule it is more convenient and quite sufficient to keep only the skeleton, after cleaning and bleaching it. The polyps will die soon after the coral is removed from the water, and the thin layer of flesh may be removed by subjecting it to the scouring action of the waves on a shallow shore for a few days. Subsequent exposure to sunlight will bleach it, especially if it is kept at alternate intervals in seawater and the sunlight. If it is not convenient to do this, the coral may be placed in a solution (dilutions of 1 in 5 to 1 in 10 are recommended) of ordinary commercial laundry bleach for 24 hours before washing and drying in the sun.

7

List of the Western Atlantic Reef Corals

THE LIST that follows includes most of the known species of true reef corals which grow on the Atlantic coasts of the American continent. They are all known to occur in less than 50 feet of water. Among them are a few rare species. Nevertheless, since they have a form sufficiently distinct to be recognized and since the purpose of this book is to provide a simple means of identification, no attempt has been made to resolve the question of varieties versus species. Also included are a number of solitary species which occur among reef corals, but which are not true reef corals themselves; these are marked with an asterisk. Also included is the stinging coral, often mistaken for a coral, which is a member of an entirely different order of coelenterates. The system of classification adopted is that of Wells and Vaughan (1944).

Below the scientific name of each species is the most appropriate common name available. It is very probable that other names, some of which might be more suitable, are also in use to greater or lesser extent.

CLASS ANTHOZOA

Order Scleractinia

Suborder Astrocoeniida

Family Astrocoeniidae	1.	*Stephanocoenia michelini* Edwards & Haime
Seriatoporidae	2.	*Madracis decactis* (Lyman)
	3.	*M. mirabilis* (Duchassaing & Michelotti)
Acroporidae	4.	*Acropora cervicornis* (Lamarck) (staghorn coral)
	5.	*A. palmata* (Lamarck) (elkhorn coral)
	6.	*A. prolifera* (Lamarck) (staghorn coral)

Suborder Fungiida

Agariciidae	7.	*Agaricia agaricites* (Linnaeus) (leaf coral)
	8.	*A. agaricites purpurea* Lesson
	9.	*A. fragilis* Dana (hat coral)
	10.	*A. nobilis* Verrill (hat coral)
Siderastreidae	11.	*Siderastrea radians* (Pallas) (starlet coral)
	12.	*S. siderea* (Ellis & Solander) (starlet coral)
	13.	*S. stellata* Verrill (starlet coral)
Poritidae	14.	*Porites astreoides* Lamarck (porous coral)
	15.	*P. branneri* Rathbun (porous coral)
	16.	*P. divaricata* Lesueur (small finger coral)

17. *P. furcata* Lamarck
(finger coral)
18. *P. porites* (Pallas)
(clubbed finger coral)
19. *P. verrilli* Rehberg
(Brazilian porous coral)

Suborder Faviida

Faviidae

20. *Favia conferta* Verrill
(grooved coral)
21. *F. fragum* (Esper)
(star coral)
22. *F. gravida* Verrill
(star coral)
23. *F. leptophylla* Verrill
(star coral)
24. *Diplora clivosa* (Ellis & Solander)
(brain coral)
25. *D. labyrinthiformis* (Linnaeus)
(brain coral)
26. *D. strigosa* (Dana)
(common brain coral)
27. *Colpophyllia amaranthus* (Houttuyn)
(rose coral)
28. *C. natans* (Houttuyn)
(brain coral)
29. *Manicina areolata* (Linnaeus)
(common rose coral)
30. *M. mayori* Wells
(Tortugas rose coral)
31. *Cladocora arbuscula* Lesueur
(tube coral)
32. *Solenastrea bournoni* Edwards & Haime
(star coral)

	33.	*S. hyades* (Dana) (lobed star coral)
	34.	*Montastrea annularis* (Ellis & Solander) (common star coral)
	35.	*M. braziliana* (Verrill) (Brazilian star coral)
	36.	*M. aperta* (Verrill)
	37.	*M. cavernosa* (Linnaeus) (large star coral)
Astrangiidae	*38.	*Astrangia solitaria* (Lesueur) (dwarf cup coral)
	*39.	*A. rathbuni* Vaughan
	*40.	*A. brasiliensis* Vaughan
	*41.	*Phyllangia americana* Edwards & Haime
Oculinidae	42.	*Oculina diffusa* Lamarck (ivory bush coral)
	43.	*O. valenciennesi* Edwards & Haime (ivory tree coral)
	44.	*O. varicosa* Lesueur (ivory tree coral)
Trochosmiliidae	45.	*Meandrina meandrites* (Linnaeus) (brain coral)
	46.	*M. brasiliensis* (Edwards & Haime) (Brazilian rose coral)
	47.	*M. danae* (Edwards & Haime)
	48.	*Dichocoenia stokesii* Edwards & Haime (star coral)
	49.	*Dendrogyra cylindrus* Ehrenberg (pillar coral)
Mussidae	50.	*Mussismilia brasiliensis* (Verrill) (Brazilian flower coral)
	51.	*M. harttii* (Verrill) (flower coral)

52. *Mussa angulosa* (Pallas)
(large flower coral)
53. *Scolymia lacera* (*Pallas*)
(mushroom coral)
54. *Isophyllastrea rigida* (Dana)
(rough star coral)
55. *Mycetophyllia lamarckiana*
(Edwards & Haime)
(large cactus coral)
56. *Isophyllia sinuosa*
(Ellis & Solander)
(cactus coral)
57. *I. multiflora* Verrill
(lesser cactus coral)

Suborder Caryophyllida

Caryophyllidae 58. *Eusmilia fastigiata* (Pallas)
(flower coral)

Suborder Dendrophyllida

Dendrophyllidae *59. *Tubastrea tenuilamellosa*
(Edwards & Haime)

CLASS HYDROZOA

Order Hydrocorallinae

Milleporidae *60. *Millepora alcicornis* Linnaeus
(false or stinging coral)

8

Identification of the Western Atlantic Reef Corals

THE CHARACTERISTICS used in the scientific classification of corals are difficult to study outside of the laboratory or without a detailed knowledge of their structure. It is possible nevertheless to identify with fair accuracy the greater number of reef corals, even without special training, by means of the simplified key which follows. The key is based upon characters which may be seen with the naked eye or with a small hand lens after the coral has been taken from the water and the flesh removed. A ruler graduated in centimeters and calipers for measuring the diameter of the coral cup are very useful aids.

Technical terms have been avoided as much as possible in the key, but it is advisable to read section 4 on the structure and habits of the living coral before attempting to use it.

The first and most obvious character to look for is the presence of typical coral cups or calices. The false or stinging coral does not have these, but instead is covered with fine pinholes.

Some adult corals remain as single cups either completely isolated or connected only by a thin plate at the very base. The majority, however, are united to form massive structures, which may be evenly dome-shaped or more irregular (Plates 19, 29, 31). Others have their cups united to form a branching structure (Plates 3, 4, 28, 34, 42, 48). The branches may each consist of a single cup (Plates 28, 48) or they may be covered with many cups. In the latter case the cups sometimes lie flush with the surface (Plate 13). In other branching corals the cups project noticeably from the surface (Plates 3, 4, 34).

The cups of some corals are well separated (Plate 37) by the general coral surface, but in others their walls are united to form a common boundary (Plates 10, 14, 17, 43). They may also join together to form elongated valleys as in the brain corals (Plates 19, 20, 21, 22). The diameter of the cup or the width of the valley from wall to wall is used as an aid to quick identification. The walls themselves may be thin, or in some cases they are wide and may develop a groove (Plate 21).

The septa or partitions which project from the walls toward the center of the cup or valley are not all of the same size, and they also vary in the distance between them. Care should be taken to count both long and short septa in determining the number of septa per centimeter. Edges of the septa may be smooth (Plates 35, 36, 39) or toothed (Plates 10, 17, 32, 41, 44) and irregular. At the inner edge of each septum there sometimes occur small plates or lobes, which are known as pali (Plate 14). In the center of the cup a simple axial rod (Plate 1) is developed in some corals. This is the columella, which varies in form from a solid rod to a more diffuse structure. In a number of corals the upper edges of the septa extend outside the boundary of the cup over the general surface of the coral between cups. This condition is known as costate (Plate 33).

Occasionally, difficulty may arise in identifying young corals. Young stages may consist of single cups, even though the adult is more complicated. Another possible source of confusion is due to the considerable variation which may take place in corals as a result of the changing nature of their surroundings. In these cases a whole series of similar forms should be examined before a definite conclusion is reached. Only rarely, however, should it be necessary to use the more technical literature listed in the bibliography.

Use of the key is simple. Starting at 1, there is a choice of two descriptions. The description which more closely fits the specimen is selected. Opposite the selected description is a number which refers to another pair of descriptions further on in the key. By determining the appropriate one of these and continuing the process, the reader will eventually arrive at the name of his specimen. To provide a quick check on the accuracy of identification, references to photographic illustrations are placed throughout the key.

Simplified Key to the Reef Corals of the Western Atlantic

1. Coral massive, branched, or plate-like. Smooth surface pierced with fine pinholes. No cups.
   Millepora alcicornis Linnaeus
   (stinging coral)

   Coral surface patterned by one or many cups with radiating septa or by grooves with parallel septa 2
2. Coral never forms branched or massive structure, but consists of a single cup 3

Coral forms a branched, massive, or encrusting structure, with many cups, which may be joined together to form grooves 7

3. The cup is large, up to 6 cm in diameter, with numerous radiating septa, toothed along their edges (Plate 41).
   Scolymia lacera (Pallas)
   (mushroom coral)

   The cup is small, less than 10 mm in diameter. Cups may occur in groups, growing on shells or rocks 4

4. Cups about 1 cm in diameter. Columella weak.
   Phyllangia americana Edwards & Haime
   (cup coral)

   Cups 5 mm or less in diameter. Columella distinct 5

5. Cups widely separated on thin encrustation.
   Astrangia brasiliensis Vaughan
   (dwarf cup coral)

   Cups more closely spaced on thicker encrustation 6

6. Inner edge of septa almost perpendicular, central cavity deep and narrow.
   Astrangia solitaria (Lesueur)
   (dwarf cup coral)

   Inner edge of septa slopes, central cavity shallow.
   Astrangia rathbuni Vaughan
   (dwarf cup coral)

7. Coral is branched (Plates 3, 4, 12, 13, 28, 34, 40, 42, 48) . . 8

   Coral is massive, leaf-like, or encrusting but never branched . 21

8. The cups only occur at the ends of the branches and branchlets (Plates 28, 40, 42, 48) 9

   The cups are scattered over entire surface of branches (Plates 1, 3, 4, 12, 13, 34) 12

9. Cups small, tubular, about 3 mm in diameter, little or no wider than branch bearing them. Colonies form loose clumps up to 6 inches in diameter (Plate 28).
   Cladocora arbuscula Lesueur
   (tube coral)

Cups over 1 cm in diameter (Plates 40, 42, 48) 10

10. Edges of septa not toothed. Cups usually oval, up to 3.5 cm in diameter, sometimes with two or three centers. Colonies form rounded masses up to 9 inches in diameter, cups having flower-like aspect (Plate 48).

Eusmilia fastigiata (Pallas)
(flower coral)

Edges of septa prominently toothed (Plates 40, 42) 11

11. Cups about 2.5 cm in diameter. Septa thin, more than 12 per cm, with slender irregular teeth (Plate 40).

Mussismilia harttii (Verrill)
(Brazilian flower coral)

Cups about 5 cm in diameter. Septa thicker, 8 per cm, with larger coarser teeth (Plate 42).

Mussa angulosa (Pallas)
(large flower coral)

12. Cups conical or cylindrical, projecting above surface of branches (Plates 3, 4, 34) 13

Cups do not project above surface of branches (Plates 1, 12, 13) 18

13. Cups form small cylindrical projections less than 2 mm wide, with perforated walls, densely crowded on branches (Plates 3, 4) 14

Cups at summit of low conical projections, solid walls, well separated (Plate 34) 16

14. Branches flattened or fan-like, like elk or moose antlers (Plate 4).

Acropora palmata (Lamarck)
(elkhorn or moosehorn coral)

Branches cylindrical (Plate 3) 15

15. Branches diverging, rarely fused together, forming open thicket-like tangles (Plate 3).

Acropora cervicornis (Lamarck)
(staghorn or deerhorn coral)

16. Coral bushy with numerous short branches, usually under 5

mm thick, frequently fusing. Cups 3-4 mm in diameter (Plate 34).

Oculina diffusa Lamarck
(ivory bush coral)

Coral more open and straggling, branches long and crooked, over 3/8 inch thick. Cups 3 mm or less in diameter 17

17. Main branches usually under 2 cm in diameter. Cups usually with depression around base. Less than 1/8 inch in diameter.

Oculina valenciennesi Edwards & Haime
(lesser ivory tree coral)

Main branches 3-5 cm in diameter. Cups up to 3.5 mm in diameter, placed upon swollen projections.

Oculina varicosa Lesueur
(larger ivory tree coral)

18. Cups separated by coral surface. Septa solid (Plate 1) 19

Cups in close contact, joined by common walls. Septa and walls porous (Plates 12, 13) 20

19. Colony forms mass of erect columnar lobes, or thick stubby branches 1-1.5 cm in diameter, often in fan-like groups. Cups separated by beaded ridges and arranged in polygonal pattern (Plate 1).

Madracis decactis (Lyman)

Colony straggling and diffuse, branchlets long and slender. Prickles or ridges between cups.

Madracis mirabilis (Duchassaing & Michelotti)

20. Branches have blunt swollen ends and are over 12 mm wide. Cups shallow, about 2 mm diameter (Plates 13, 14).

Porites porites (Pallas)
(clubbed finger coral)

Branches not swollen at tips and are under 12 mm wide. Cups deeper, about 1.5 mm diameter (Plate 12).

Porites furcata Lamarck
(finger coral)

21. Coral flattened, forming clumps of thick, flat blades, or clusters of delicate leaf-like projections, or saucer-like plates

fastened to the bottom by a central stalk or along one edge (Plates 5, 7, 8) 22
Coral encrusting, massive, or top-shaped, but never leaf-like . 25

22. Cups on both sides of plates (Plates 5, 6).
Agaricia agaricites (Linnaeus)
(leaf coral)
Cups on one side of plates only (Plates 7, 8) 23

23. Coral is thin and broadly cup-like, attached by short stalk (Plate 8).
Agaricia fragilis Dana
(hat coral)
Coral is thick and usually plate-like, attached by one edge or by large area of lower surface (Plate 7) 24

24. Cups isolated and in groups of 2-6, sometimes more, widely spaced, inclined to outer edge of frond, forming bracket-like ridges on inner side. Extensions of septa beyond edge of cup alternately large and small (Plate 7).
Agaricia nobilis Verrill
(hat coral)
Cups isolated and in series, crowded, sunken between sharp ridges. Septal extensions uniform in size.
Agaricia agaricites purpurea
Lesson

25. Coral usually less than 6 inches in diameter, circular or oval, top-shaped, with short conical stalk when young, unattached when fully developed (Plates 25, 26) 26
Coral forms spheroidal or irregular boulders or heads, sometimes rather flattened, sometimes with lobes or columns. Permanently attached (Plates 11, 16, 18, 19, 24, 29, 31, 38) 28

26. Edges of septa are toothed, bottom of valley has spongy twisted strands (Plate 27).
Manicina areolata (Linnaeus)
(rose coral)
Edges of septa smooth, bottom of valley has prominent laminar plates 27

27. Upper surface of coral moderately or strongly arched. Lower surface has toothed ridges extending downward from ends of septa (Plate 36).

    Meandrina brasiliensis (Edwards & Haime)
    (Brazilian rose coral)

    Upper surface gently arched or nearly flat. Lower surface has ridges only near outer edge.

    Meandrina danae (Edwards & Haime)

28. Surface of coral covered with complicated pattern of elongated sinuous more or less branching valleys (Plates 19-24, 35, 39, 45) 29

    Surface of coral covered with circular, oval, or elongated cups not united in long valleys (Plates 1, 2, 9, 15, 17, 18) . . 40

29. Coral forms thick erect, straight, or knobbed pillars sometimes of very large size (Plates 38, 39).

    Dendrogyra cylindrus Ehrenberg
    (pillar coral)

    Coral forms flattened or rounded boulders. No pillars 30

30. Edges of septa not toothed 31

    Edges of septa toothed 32

31. Septa thick and coarse. Septa of adjacent valleys do not meet. Short flattened plates in bottom of valleys (Plate 39). (Form without pillars)

    Dendrogyra cylindrus Ehrenberg
    (pillar coral)

    Septa thinner and sharp edged. Septa of adjacent valleys meet in sharp zigzag line on top of separating wall. Continuous series of long flattened plates in bottom of valleys (Plate 35).

    Meandrina meandrites (Linnaeus)
    (brain coral)

32. Wall separating adjacent valleys distinctly double 33

    Walls not double, though there may be a shallow groove . . . 35

33. Spongy twisted material in bottom of valley.
Manicina mayori (Wells)
(Tortugas rose coral)
No twisted material in bottom of valley 34
34. Coral usually less than 6 inches across, often with broad stalk underneath. Valley more than 12 mm deep, usually. Septa 11 per cm (Plate 24).
Colpophyllia amaranthus
(Houttuyn)
Coral may reach large size. Valley less than 12 mm deep. Septa 9 per cm (Plate 23).
Colpophyllia natans (Houttuyn)
35. Thin toothed vertical plates run lengthwise along floor of valleys (Plates 44, 45).
Mycetophyllia lamarckiana
(Edwards & Haime)
Spongy material in floor of valleys. No plates 36
36. Valleys long and sinuous, less than 1 cm wide. Septal teeth fine, numerous (Plates 20, 21, 22) 37
Valleys shorter, lobed, more than 1.5 cm wide. Septal teeth coarse, fewer (Plates 46, 47) 39
37. Coral forms flattened uneven masses with knobs or hillocks near center. Walls between valleys have sharp crest, no groove. Septa more than 30 per cm (Plates 19, 20).
Diploria clivosa (Ellis & Solander)
(knobbed brain coral)
Coral forms more regular spheroidal or dome-shaped masses. Walls more rounded or flattened, sometimes with groove . . 38
38. Walls always grooved on top (Plate 21).
Diploria labyrinthiformis
(Linnaeus)
(brain coral)
Walls not grooved except rarely at edge of coral (Plate 22).
Diploria strigosa (Dana)
(common brain coral)

39. Valleys average 2.5 cm wide. Septa about 8 to the cm (Plate 46).

Isophyllia sinuosa (Ellis & Solander)
(cactus coral)

Valleys average 1.5 cm wide. Septa about 12 to the cm (Plate 47).

Isophyllia multiflora Verrill
(lesser cactus coral)

40. Cups tubular, projecting nearly half inch from surface of coral. Coral light and spongy. Living coral bright orange in color.

Tubastrea tenuilamellosa
(Edwards & Haime)

Cups not tubular, little or no projection. Coral dense and heavy 41

41. Diameter of cups more than 1 cm 42

Diameter of cups averages less than 1 cm 43

42. Septa thin, with numerous slender teeth pointing horizontally.

Mussismilia brasiliensis (Verrill)
(Brazilian flower coral)

Septa thick, edges with 6-8 coarse teeth pointing obliquely upward.

Isophyllastrea rigida (Dana)
(rough star coral)

43. Coral porous, cups always with common walls, never separated (Plates 9, 15) 44

Coral not porous, cups mostly separate but occasionally with fused walls (Plates 1, 2, 17, 18) 49

44. Cups have 12 septa, composed of 1-4 vertical spines, loosely united and perforated by pores (Plate 15) 45

Cups wider, 24-48 or more septa not made up of distinct spines, plate-like with beaded edges (Plates 9, 10) 47

45. Cups 0.9-1.2 mm in diameter.

Porites branneri Rathbun
(porous coral)

Cups larger, 1.2-1.5 mm in diameter 46

46. Cups shallow, walls less than 0.4 mm thick (Plate 15).
Porites astreoides Lamarck
(porous coral)

Cups deeper, walls about 0.4 mm thick.
Porites verrilli Rehberg
(Brazilian porous coral)

47. Cups not regularly pentagonal, especially near edge of coral, 2-3 mm wide, 6 mm long, sometimes united in short, meandering series (Plate 11).
Siderastrea stellata Verrill
(starlet coral)

Cups more regularly pentagonal up to 5 mm wide (Plates 9, 10.) 48

48. Cups 2.5-3.5 mm in diameter. Septa with inner margins almost perpendicular so that pit is narrow and straight sided (Plate 9).
Siderastrea radians (Pallas)
(starlet coral)

Cups 3.5-5.0 mm in diameter. Septal margins slope gently so that pit is shallow (Plate 10).
Siderastrea siderea (Ellis & Solander)
(starlet coral)

49. Cups have rod-like column in center (Plate 1) 50
Cups have lamellar structure in center (Plate 37) 51

50. Septa usually 24, extending as ridges beyond cup. Cups 2.6-3.0 mm in diameter (Plate 2).
Stephanocoenia michelini Edwards & Haime

Septa usually 10, not extending as ridges beyond cup. Cups separated by lines of beads. Cups 1.5-2.5 mm in diameter (Plate 1).
(Lobate form)
Madracis decactis (Lyman)

51. Cups crowded, joined by fused or common walls 52

Cups more or less crowded but walls always separate 54

52. Common walls are distinctly double. Cups round or oval, but becoming lobed when polycentric, 5-8 mm in diameter.
    Favia leptophylla Verrill

    Common walls not double (Plates 17, 18) 53

53. Cups 4.5-6.5 mm in diameter, circular or oval, lobed or polygonal when older but never elongated or joined in series (Plates 16, 17).
    Favis fragum (Esper)
    (star coral)

    Cups 3-4 mm in diameter, often elongated to 20 mm or more in short meandering series (Plate 18).
    Favia conferta Verrill
    (grooved coral)

54. Cups smaller than 6 mm wide but may be elongated to 30 mm long (Plates 29-33, 37) 55

    Cups always roughly circular, 6 mm or larger in diameter . . 57

55. Cups 3-5 mm wide but most are oval or elongated 56

    Cups 2-3.5 mm in diameter, always circular or polygonal but never elongated 59

56. Septa with toothed edges and thorny sides. Cups up to 8 mm long.
    Favia gravida Verrill
    (star coral)

    Septa minutely serrated, edges granular, not thorny. Cups sometimes almost circular but usually elongated to about 10 mm, occasionally to 30 mm (Plate 37).
    Dichocoenia stokesii Edwards & Haime
    (star coral)

57. All septa extend as ridges or coral walls outside cups (Plate 37) 58

    Septa of fourth cycle lower than first three and not extending beyond cup.
    Montastrea aperta (Verrill)

58. Coral between cups not blistered in appearance (Plate 33).
Montastrea cavernosa (Linnaeus)
(large star coral)

Coral between cups strongly blistered in appearance, partly hiding extensions of septa.
Montastrea braziliana Verrill
(Brazilian star coral)

59. Cups 3-3.5 mm in diameter. Septa do not extend as ridges beyond cup. Coral often with rounded lobes on upper surface (Plates 29, 30).
Solenastrea hyades (Dana)
(lobed star coral)

Cups 2-2.5 mm in diameter. Septa extend beyond cups (Plate 32) 60

60. Septal extensions prominent, serrated. No blistered appearance between cups. Coral forms huge rounded boulders (Plates 31, 32).
Montastrea annularis (Ellis & Solander)
(common star coral)

Septal extensions present but inconspicuous. Blistered appearance between cups. Coral forms smaller heads 1-2 feet in diameter.
Solenastrea bournoni Edwards & Haime

9

Description of the Western Atlantic Reef Corals

THE FOLLOWING brief descriptions of the corals found upon the reefs of the western Atlantic Ocean are written primarily for those who have no acquaintance with the technicalities of coral taxonomy. The geographical locations given are not necessarily inclusive. A technical description, appended for the use of students, is set in smaller type.

Since the corals may have been referred to by other names in previous descriptions, the more important of these are indicated together with the publication in which they appeared. All references to publications are made by placing the date of publication in parentheses after the author's name. The full title and source will be found under this reference in the bibliography. No attempt has been made to give the detailed synonymy of the corals described, but the name adopted is, as far as can be determined, that accepted by the most recent authors.

Following the synonym will be found a reference to the best available published description, though not necessarily the most complete. In selecting it, the quality of illustrations and the availability of the literature has been taken into account. Often the original description may be the most complete, but nearly as often this is hidden in journals that are to be found in very few libraries.

1. *Stephanocoenia michelini* (Edwards and Haime), (Plate 2).

Also *Stephanocoenia intersepta* Vaughan (1919). Also *Plesiastrea goodei* Verrill (1902).

Described by Vaughan (1919), page 357.

Polyps brown. Coral appears very similar to *Siderastrea radians.* Forms rounded boulders under 1 foot in diameter. Rather porous. Cups close together but not always touching, and between 2 and 3 mm in diameter. Radial septa smooth or very finely toothed. Distinguished from *Siderastrea radians* by the presence of lobes or pali at the inner edges of the septa.

Grows throughout the West Indies, the Bahamas, Florida, and Bermuda, but not very commonly recognized, possibly because of its resemblance to *Siderastrea radians* when alive.

> Massive, subhemispherical. Plocoid or subcerioid. Sometimes costate. Calices 2 to 3 mm in diameter. Septa in three cycles. Exsert. Primaries and secondaries with well-developed pali. Tertiaries thin and shorter. Septal margins entire or finely dentate. Columella same height as pali, in form of a compressed style. Thin, subhorizontal endothecal dissepiments about 0.5 mm apart.

2. *Madracis decatis* (Lyman), (Plate 1).

Described by Verrill (1902), page 108.

Polyp yellow to purple-brown in color with white tips to tentacles and lining mouth. Coral forms thin encrustations on rock, sometimes growing out into sparse branches or lobes. Usually under 6 inches. Cups do not touch, angular or circular with beaded boundary, about 2 mm in diameter. Common in Bermuda and found throughout the Bahamas and the West Indies.

Thinly encrusting, irregularly massive or lobulated or in short, stout branches. Plocoid. Beaded. Ridges bounding calices. Noncostate. Smooth septa, somewhat reduced. Columella styliform, well-developed. Peritheca extensive, nonporous. Septa usually 10, sometimes eight.

3. *Madracis mirabilis* (Duchassaing and Michelotti).

Also *Axhelia mirabilis* Vaughan (1902).

Differs from *M. decactis* in having prickles or ridges between cups instead of rows of beads and in longer, more slender branches.

4. *Acropora cervicornis* (Lamarck), (Plate 3).

Also *Acropora muricata* (Vaughan 1919). Also *Isopora muricata* (Vaughan 1901).

Discussed by Vaughan (1901), page 312 and (1919), page 482.

Brownish yellow. Coral forms loosely branched colony with small tubular cup protruding over entire surface. May grow to 10 feet high. Abundant in Florida, the Bahamas, and the West Indies, but not in Bermuda or Brazil.

Ramose colonies, branches consisting of an axial corallite with radial corallites budded from it. Corallites protuberant, tubular or pariform, 1 to 3 mm long, with porous walls. Synapticulothecate. Septa well-developed. Pseudo-costate.

5. *Acropora palmata* (Lamarck), (Plate 4).

Also *Isopora muricata* forma palmata (Vaughan 1900).

Discussed by Vaughan (1901), page 313 and (1919), page 482.

Brownish yellow. Coral forms flat frond-like branches resembling somewhat the horns of an elk. Other characteristics similar to *A. cervicornis*, of which it has been considered a variety. Found throughout Florida Keys, the Bahamas, and the West Indies.

Corallites similar to *A. cervicornis.* Branches flabelliform or frond-like, flattened in more or less horizontal plane.

6. *Acropora prolifera* (Lamarck).

Also *Isopora muricata* forma prolifera (Vaughan 1901).

Discussed by Vaughan (1901), page 313 and (1919), page 482.

Brownish yellow. Similar to *Acropora cervicornis* with branches joining where they cross so as to form flattened plates. Has been considered merely a variety of *Acropora cervicornis*, which is intermediate between that species and *Acropora palmata,* also considered a variety. The validity of these species is discussed by Vaughan. Found throughout Florida Keys, the Bahamas, and the West Indies.

Corallites similar to *A. cervicornis* Branches more crowded, however, tending to fuse into flabelliform growths.

7. *Agaricia agaricites* (Linnaeus), (Plates 5, 6).

Also *Agaricia crassa* Verrill, (Verrill 1902), also *Agaricia purpurea* Lesson, (Verrill 1902).

Described by Verrill (1902), pages 140-150 and by Vaughan (1919), page 427.

Chocolate to purple-brown. Short white tentacles. Coral forms more or less erect fronds covered with cups on both faces, as a rule. Sometimes due to growth conditions (see Vaughan), the fronds may be reduced and an almost massive, slightly lobed form result (variety *crassa*). Sometimes the cups may be restricted to one face (variety *purpurea*). Cups arranged in parallel groups of varying lengths separated by slightly projecting walls. Common on the Florida reefs, in the Bahamas, and southward to Brazil.

Coral usually foliaceous or frondous, but sometimes massive or encrusting. Fronds usually bifacial, irregular 5 to 20 mm thick.

Calices arranged in groups between more or less parallel collines, small and shallow, about 2 to 3 mm. Septa low, up to 36, finely serrulate. Costate. Synapticulae between septa.

8. *Agaricia agaricites purpurea* Lesson.

See *Agaricia agaricites.*

9. *Agaricia fragilis* Dana.

Described by Verrill (1902), page 142.

Generally similar to *A. agaricites,* with the following differences. Coral grows out into cup-shaped or saucer-shaped fronds, which are thin and delicate. Usually up to 6 inches across and with cups on upper surface only. Ridges between cups generally long and low. Cups about 2 mm across. The only Bermuda species of *Agaricia.* Also off Florida Keys.

Pedicelled, with broad, thin, saucer-shaped or cup-shaped frond, unifacial, about 3 mm thick. Rarely over 150 mm. Calices small, about 2 mm, generally with edges elevated. Septa and costae thin and finely serrulate. Collines vary, but usually long, regular, rounded, and little elevated, forming long concentric series of calices. Septa up to 24. Collines about 20 mm apart.

10. *Agaricia nobilis* Verrill, (Plate 7).

Described by Verrill (1902), page 150.

Grows in thin fronds or cups, not as small or delicate as those of *A. fragilis,* but thinner than those of *A. agaricites.* Cups on upper surface only. Under surface covered with fine ridges. Chocolate to purple brown in color. The cups are in small groups of three or four. They are separated by walls which are strongly inclined toward the edge of the frond, so that they appear as if supported in brackets. As many as 48 septa in each cup. Cups about 4 mm across. Not common. Florida reefs, the Bahamas, and the West Indies.

Pedicelled with rounded, concave, or flat fronds varying from 1 to 5 mm thick. Costal striae cover under surface. Calices on upper surface in small groups of three to six, separated by prominent, fairly short, curved collines set at an acute angle to the frond and facing toward edge of the frond. Calices up to 5 mm, fairly deep, with 36 to 48 finely serrulate septa. Septo-costae about 10 mm.

11. *Siderastrea radians* (Pallas), (Plate 15).

Described by Vaughan (1919), page 439.

Corals form rounded or pebble-shaped stones up to 1 foot or more across, but sometimes when young form encrustations. Grayish to brown in color. Cups small, about 3 mm, and angular. Inner edges of septa perpendicular, cavity of cup deep and narrow. Distinguished from *S. siderea* by smaller cup and deep narrow cavity. Very common in shallow water in Bermuda, Florida, the Bahamas, and the West Indies to South America and Colón.

Spheroidal or hemispherical masses up to 500 mm in diameter. Often encrusting or irregular when young, or loose on bottom. Cerioid. Calices 2.5 to 3.5 mm, angular. Septa 36 to 40, four unequal cycles, first two very distinct from others, last cycle incomplete. Larger septa slightly exsert, serrulate, inner edges perpendicular. Columella small and papillose.

12. *Siderastrea siderea* (Ellis and Solander), (Plate 10).

Described by Vaughan (1919), page 443.

Larger masses than *S. radians,* sometimes over 2 feet. Cups 4 to 5 mm across. Septal margins slope more than *S. radians* so that cup is larger and shallower. Septa 50 to 60. Common on Florida reefs, Bahamas, West Indies, and Bermuda.

Hemispherical masses up to 2 or 3 feet in diameter. Calices up to 4 to 5 mm, sometimes 6 mm in diameter, wall slightly raised. Three or four rows of synapticulae on each side of wall between septa. Septa in five cycles, last cycle incomplete. Less difference in size of septa than *S. radians.* Septal margins more sloping and more finely dentate. Columella small.

13. *Siderastrea stellata* Verrill.

Described by Vaughan (1919), page 440.

Similar to *S. radians,* but cups deeper and more irregular. Found only in Brazil, where it is widely distributed on the Abrolhos Reef and at Bahia.

Calices irregular 2 to 3 mm wide and up to 6 mm or more long. Cerioid. Four cycles of septa, last cycle incomplete. Inner margins of septa very steep, more coarsely dentate than *S. radians.* Columella finely papillate and less developed than in *S. radians.*

14. *Porites astreoides* Lamarck, (Plate 19).

Described by Verrill (1902), page 160.

Usually yellowish brown. Forms rounded masses, covered with small bumps and growing up to more than 2 feet. Cups from 1.25 to 1.50 mm in diameter. Septa have small rough teeth and are porous, 12 in number. Abundant from Florida reefs and Bahamas to Brazil. Also present in Bermuda.

Encrusting when young, massive subnodular, calices 1.25 to 1.50 mm in diameter. Twelve septa, porous, rarely distinct pali. Columella very small, porous. Calices larger, deeper, and with higher and more distinct walls than *P. porites.*

15. *Porites branneri* Rathbun.

Described by Verrill (1902), page 162.

Very porous rounded masses up to 6 inches, formed by thick encrustations over stones or dead coral. Small cups about 1 mm across. Inner edges of septa join to form a ring. Found on Brazilian reefs and possibly in the West Indies.

Thick, rounded encrustations, 3 to 6 inches, covering dead coral. Calices small and shallow, crowded, polygonal, with thin fenestrated walls, diameter 0.9 to 1.2 mm. Septa 12, narrow, spiny and fenestrated, inner edges uniting to form columelliform ring. Pali, when present, three to five, slender, erect.

16. *Porites divaricata* Lesueur.

Discussed by Vaughan (1901), page 316.

Although this is probably a variety of *P. furcata* or *P. porites* it is distinct in appearance. The branches are much smaller than *P. furcata,* under 6 mm in diameter with no tapering or dilation along the length of a branch. Florida, Bahamas, and the West Indies.

Branches less than 6 mm in diameter, same at proximal and distal end, calices very shallow, 2 mm in diameter. Wall narrow, rather flat or subacute.

17. *Porites furcata* Lamarck, (Plate 12).

Discussed by Vaughan (1901), page 316.

Branching colonies, branches thicker than *P. divaricata,* but without the swollen ends of *P. porites.* Cups smaller than in *P. porites.* Florida, Bahamas, and the West Indies.

Ramose. Branches vary in diameter, about 10 mm, ends never clubbed. Calices about 1.5 mm in diameter, usually only five pali.

18. *Porites porites* (Pallas), (Plates 13, 14).

Also *Porites polymorpha* Link, (Verrill 1902), also *Porites clavaria* Lamarck, (Vaughan).

Described by Vaughan (1901), page 314.

This name has been used to include all the branched species of *Porites.* The question of species versus varieties is discussed by Vaughan (1901).

Branched, larger branches than *P. furcata,* with ends swollen and blunt. Columella and pali usually present. Found throughout the western Atlantic reef areas, except Brazil.

Colony forms thick clumps of irregular stout branches, swollen at ends. Calices shallow, deeper on ends of branches, 2 mm in diameter. Columella represented by tubercle and surrounded by six pali which are less developed in the calices at ends of branches. Septa perforate.

19. *Porites verrilli* Rehberg.

Described by Verrill (1902), page 161.

Massive, similar to *P. astreoides* but larger and more solid. Cups deeper, and separated by thicker, more solid and prominent walls. Common on coast of Brazil.

Larger and more solid than *P. astreoides.* Calices deeper. Walls more solid, thicker, and prominent. Pali rudimentary or absent. Columella large, solid, and tuberculate, sometimes with slight styliform projection.

20. *Favia conferta* Verrill.

Described by Verrill (1868), page 355.

Discussed by Vaughan (1901), page 304.

Encrusting masses, never very large. Yellowish brown in color. Cups irregular in shape, also short valleys separated by narrow walls. Septa similar to *F. fragum.* Only in Brazil.

Encrusting or submassive up to a few inches. Intratentacular budding. Monostomodoeal polyps or short series, forming curved but not sinuous valleys, separated by small narrow collines. Otherwise similar to *F. fragum.* Costate, septa exsert. Septal margins irregularly dentate. Columella parietal, spongy.

21. *Favia fragum* (Esper), (Plates 16, 17).

Discussed by Vaughan (1901), page 303.

Forms small crusts on other rocks or small rounded pebbles an inch or two long. Light yellow to brown. Cups angular, circular, or oval, under 6.5 mm across. Septa have irregular teeth on margins. Bermuda, Florida, the Bahamas, and the West Indies. Common in shallow water.

Encrusting or capuliform masses or subhemispherical, up to 50 mm. Calices circular, angular, or elliptical. Under 6.5 mm in diameter. Average 4.5 mm or less. Walls 1.5 mm or more.

Septa from three to nearly four complete cycles, 36 to 40, margins irregularly dentate. Costae acute, dentate. Columella large, spongy.

22. *Favia gravida* Verrill.

Described by Verrill (1868), page 354.

Similar to *F. fragum.* Walls of cups stand out above surface and separate from each other. Cups oval or deformed by crowding, never elongated into valleys. Brazil only.

Plocoid. Small, encrusting, or subhemispherical. Margins of calicinal walls projecting beyond perithecal surface. Circular or oval calices, never much elongated, similar to *F. fragum.* Four complete cycles of septa.

23. *Favia leptophylla* (Verrill).

Also *Orbicella aperta* Verrill.

Verrill (1868), page 353.

Distinguished from *F. fragum* and *F. gravida* by more massive growth up to 2 feet. Cups about 6 mm. Walls of cups thin, separated by blistered coral. Septa project well over top of wall. Confined to Brazil.

Massive, up to 2 feet. Plocoid. True walls thin with loose vesicular exotheca between calices. Calices 6 mm. Septa rather few, thin, prominent, and exsert. Interseptal loculi wide and deep.

24. *Diploria clivosa* (Ellis and Solander), (Plates 19, 20).

Also *Meandra clivosa,* (Vaughan 1919, Verrill 1902), also *Meandrina clivosa,* (Matthai 1928).

Described by Matthai (1928), pages 71-76.

Greenish brown in grooves, chocolate colored over walls, tentacles bright green, white toward tips. Rather large, heavy, but low growth with irregular knobs over surface. Valleys not all connected together, shallow and narrow, very winding except at edge. Walls never grooved. Septa thin and close together. Florida and West Indies, but not Bermuda or Brazil.

Corallum heavy, spreading. Calicinal surface uneven with short irregular hillocks. Valleys discontinuous, width up to 6 mm, average 3.75 mm, depth 3.5 to 4 mm, usually very sinuous but straight toward edge of corallum. Colline rather sharp at summit, 1 to 1.5 mm thick, never grooved. Septa thin, 30 to 40, average 35 per cm, in two alternate series. Principal septa with rather thick paliform lobes. All septa continuous over colline, exsert ends angular. Columella well developed, of closely twisted trabeculae about w to 1.2 mm in width.

25. *Diploria labyrinthiformis* (Linnaeus), (Plate 21).

Also *Meandrina labyrinthiformis,* (Matthai 1928), also *Meandra labyrinthiformis,* (Verrill 1902).

Described by Matthai (1928), pages 63-71.

Color bright orange-yellow to brownish-yellow. Forms large, rounded boulders. Valleys twisting, narrower and deeper than *D. strigosa,* nearly all interconnected. Walls thick, with a longitudinal groove, which is sometimes wider and deeper even than the valleys. Septa thicker and not quite so closely arranged as *D. strigosa.* Abundant in area behind reef edge, Bermuda, Bahamas, Florida, and the West Indies. Not found in Brazil.

Hemispherical, evenly convex, heavy masses up to 6 or 8 feet in diameter. Valley very sinuous except at edge of corallum, almost continuous, width up to 8 mm, average 5 mm, depth 5 mm. Colline thick, vesicular peritheca up to 20 mm, average 8 mm. Ambulacrum invariably grooved up to 22 mm in width, average 5 mm and up to 12 mm deep, average 6 mm. Septa 14 to 17 per cm, nearly all meeting columella, thicker than *D. strigosa.* Broad paliform lobes. Close, blunt, septal teeth, uppermost directed obliquely upward. Principal septa exsert 1 mm, with costae. Columella well developed of thin, closely twisted trabeculae.

26. *Diploria strigosa* (Dana), (Plate 22).

Also *Platygyra viridis* (Lesueur), Vaughan 1901, also *Meandra cerebrum* (Ellis and Solander), Verrill 1902, also *Meandra strigosa* (Dana), Vaughan 1919, also *Meandrina cerebrum* (Ellis and Solander), Matthai (1928).

Described by Matthai (1928), pages 55-63.

Dull yellow to greenish brown in color. Dome-shaped masses, smaller than *D. labyrinthiformis.* Valleys twisting, not all interconnected, wider and deeper than *D. clivosa.* Walls between valleys wider than *D. clivosa,* but rarely grooved as in *D. labyrinthiformis.* If present, grooves narrow and shallow, and usually at edge of coral. Septa continue over the walls. Bermuda, Florida, the Bahamas, and the West Indies.

Hemispherical, evenly convex. Valleys sinuous, discontinuous, up to 9 mm wide, average 6 mm, about 5 mm deep. Colline up to 4.5 mm thick, average 2.5 mm. Septa 15 to 20 per cm. Paliform lobes. Septal margins dentate, sides spinulose. Septa exsert and arched over colline. Colline rarely with shallow, narrow grooves at edge of corallum. Columella, closely twisted trabeculae.

27. *Colpophyllia amaranthus* (Houttuyn).

Described by Matthai (1928), pages 107-109.

Small and light, slightly convex mass with short stalk beneath. Valleys green, walls brown. Valleys fairly short and straight, not interconnected, grooved above with thin boundary ridges. Florida and West Indies.

Small, massive, vesicular, light, and slightly convex. Short stalk beneath. Valleys discontinuous and fairly straight, often short, width 15 to 20 mm, up to 35 mm at edge of corallum. Depth of valley 15 mm average, up to 30 mm, shallower between centers. Colline at base up to 20 mm, average 10 mm, swollen by vesicular endotheca, grooved above. Groove about 2 mm wide, 1 mm deep, bounded by thin plates of original thecae. Septa 10 to 12 per cm, six or seven meeting columella, notch in septum simulates paliform lobe. Slightly exsert, rarely meeting in colline groove. Columella rudimentary, columellar centers sometimes connected by thin toothed septal lamellae. Costae on noncalicinal surface.

28. *Colpophyllia natans* (Houttuyn), (Plate 23).

Described by Matthai (1928), pages 101-107.

Large, light convex mass. Valleys more or less interconnected and winding, shallower than *C. amaranthus.* Wall grooved as in *C. amaranthus.* Valleys green, walls brown. Florida, Bahamas, and West Indies.

Large massive, vesicular, light convex masses. No stalk. Valleys sinuous, usually continuous, width 15 to 20 mm up to 30 to 40 mm at edge, depth up to 17 mm, average 11, shallower between centers. Colline thickened at base to 22 mm, average 17 mm. Septa eight or nine per cm, five or six meeting columella. Otherwise similar to *C. amaranthus.*

29. *Manicina areolata* (Linnaeus), (Plates 25, 26, 27).

Described by Matthai (1928), pages 80-91.

Yellow to brown with greenish valley, tentacles transparent with white tips. Form varies, usually roughly oval with narrow ends and flattish upper surface and converging to a short stalk below. Never more than about 6 inches long. Valley branches out into side arms, up to 1 inch wide. Septa seen under lens have fine holes, about 18 to the centimeter and thinner than in *M. mayori.* Very common in Florida, the Bahamas, and the West Indies in shallow water.

Corallum narrow toward ends, small. Upper surface flat or convex, sometimes lobular, underneath with central short stalk. Valley continuous with median straight portion and paired lateral branches or sinuous, width up to 24 mm, usually 12 to 15 mm, depth up to 21 mm, usually 8 mm. Colline averages 3.5 mm, thick up to 9 mm, with narrow shallow grooves when thick. Septa thin, 15 to 20 in one cm, six to nine meeting columella. Principals have upper two-thirds narrow, and lower part raised into high, broad, convex, or rounded paliform lobes. Perforate. Sides spinulose. Exsert ends meet in notches in middle of colline. Columella up to 4 mm thick. Costae narrow and thin about 1 mm apart at margin of corallum, covered by thin epitheca.

30. *Manicina mayori* Wells.

Also *Manicina gyrosa* (Ellis and Solander), (Matthai 1828, Vaughan 1919, Verrill 1902).

Described by Matthai (1928), pages 91-94.

Color similar to *M. areolata.* Not narrow at ends and larger than *M. areolata.* No central stalk. Valley not completely interconnected, long and winding, about same size as *M. areolata.* Wall thinner, septa thicker, about 12 to the centimeter, without holes. Found at Dry Tortugas, Florida.

Massive, not narrow at ends, heavy, large. No central stalk. Discontinuous valley, long and sinuous, sometimes straight, about 12 mm wide up to 20 mm at edge, about 10 mm deep. Colline about 2 mm. Septa 12 per cm, majority meeting columella. Upper two-thirds narrow, lower part arched to simulate paliform lobes. Not perforate. Exsert ends meet in groove of colline. Columella 2.5 to 3 mm thick. Costae about 1 mm apart and sometimes covered by thin epitheca.

31. *Cladocora arbuscula* Lesueur, (Plate 28).

Small, densely branching form, each short branch ending in a cup. Cups about 3.5 mm in diameter, branches slightly larger. Branches with fine longitudinal ridges continuous with the septa. Florida, the Bahamas, and the West Indies.

Small, densely branching phaceloid corallum, arising by extratentacular budding. Corallite about 4 mm in diameter, calices 3 to 3.5 mm. Finely dentate septa, usually about 36, paliform lobes merging with papillose columella. Low ridges on surface of corallite corresponding to septa.

32. *Solenastrea bournoni* Edwards and Haime.

Described by Vaughan (1919), page 399.

Coral forms domes or rounded pebbles up to 1 foot in diameter, sometimes with irregular bumps on the surface. Cups, smaller than *S. hyades,* about 2 mm in diameter and separated by about 1 mm. Low ridges extend from the septa part way across the space between cups, which is somewhat blistered. Florida and West Indies.

Corallum hemispherical or spheroidal, uniformly rounded or

with gibbosities. Calices with slightly elevated margins, 2 to 2.5 mm in diameter, and about half this distance apart. Costae short. Exotheca vesicular. Septa thin, in three cycles, tertiaries alone not reaching columella. Pali thin and rather wide before first two cycles. Septal surfaces finely granulate, imperforate, small columella.

33. *Solenastrea hyades* (Dana), (Plates 29, 30).

Also *Orbicella excelsa* Dana, (Verrill 1902).

Discussed by Vaughan (1919), page 395.

Yellow brown. Grows in lobed masses or irregular crusts. Cups about 3 mm across with rims slightly raised above the surface. Cups almost touching or separated by as much as 3 mm. Septa do not extend across spaces between cups, which may be more or less blistered in appearance. Florida reefs, Bahamas, and West Indies.

Calices nearly circular, but angular when crowded, 3 to 3.5 mm in diameter, borders often slightly elevated above exotheca. Calices sometimes touching or separated by as much as 2 to 3 mm. Walls thin, costae thickened, minutely serrulate, and never extending across exothecal spaces. Exotheca smooth or vesicular. Septa 12 to 24, 12 extend to columella. Those of third cycle bend toward and join the larger ones. Septa thin at columella, thickened at wall, inner edge serrulate, sides roughly granulated. Small paliform lobes. Columella small, of small, twisted, septal processes.

34. *Montastrea annularis* (Ellis and Solander), (Plates 31, 32).

Also *Orbicella annularis,* (Vaughan 1919), also *Orbicella hispidula,* (Verrill 1902), also *Orbicella acropora* (Linnaeus), (Vaughan 1901).

Discussed by Vaughan (1919), page 365.

Grows into boulders 5 feet or more across, forming one of the principal reef-forming corals of the West Indies. Sometimes more encrusting or more irregular in shape. Yellow-brown. Cups circular, 2 to 2.5 mm in diameter and an average of 1 mm apart. Rims slightly projecting. Septa prolonged across space between cups. Florida, the Bahamas, the West Indies, and Bermuda.

Calices more or less circular, diameter varies, 2 mm to 2.5 mm, margins more or less raised above exotheca, 0.5 to 2 mm apart. Costae corresponding to all septa, edges dentate, those of adjoining calices meeting. Septa in three complete cycles, those of first two equal, fusing with columella, tertiaries shorter, inner edges free. Margins of first two cycles exsert. Septal margins dentate, sides finely granulate. Columella well developed from interlacing septal processes, one-third diameter of calice. Endothecal dissepiments thin, exothecal dissepiments thick, both horizontal.

35. *Montastrea braziliana* (Verrill).

Also *Orbicella braziliana,* (Verrill 1902), also *Orbicella cavernosa* (Quelch 1886).

Forms rounded masses up to 2 feet in diameter. Differs only from *M. cavernosa* in having strongly blistered appearance between cups and in more uniform thickening of septa. Brazil only.

According to Quelch, this differs from *O. cavernosa* only by the highly vesicular exotheca, which hides the costae, and in the uniform thickening of the septa.

36. *Montastrea aperta* (Verrill).

Also *Heliastrea aperta* (Verrill).

Discussed by Verrill (1867), page 356.

Forms rounded masses up to 1 foot or more in diameter. Cups about same size as *M. cavernosa* (7 to 8 mm in diameter), projecting slightly above surface. Septa of fourth cycle lower than other three and do not project beyond edge of cup. More cellular in texture than *M. cavernosa,* septa thinner and more acute at summit.

37. *Montastrea cavernosa* (Linnaeus), (Plate 33).

Also *Orbicella cavernosa,* (Vaughan, 1919 and Verrill, 1902).

Described by Vaughan (1919), page 380.

Forms boulders which may be over 5 feet across. Large

cups, average 8 mm in diameter, usually projecting above surface. Septa prolonged into space between cups. Rare in Bermuda but common in Florida, the Bahamas, and the West Indies.

Corallum massive, growing to considerable size, upper surface flat, irregularly convex, or domed. Calices more or less elevated, 5 to 11 mm in diameter, close together or separated as much as 6 mm. Costae well developed, denticulate, rounded, about 48. Septa 48, exsert, serrulate, in four cycles, those of first three reach columella, others may be reduced or lacking. Columella well developed, broad, with a papillary upper surface.

38. *Astrangia solitaria* (Lesueur).

Described by Vaughan (1901), page 298.

Cups single, growing attached to base of larger corals or to dead rock, sometimes with thin encrustation connecting bases of several cups. Cups tubular, about 6 mm tall and 4 mm in diameter. Most of septa with toothed edges. Septa prolonged as low ridges down side of cup. Not strictly a reef coral, but found in reefs from Bermuda to Brazil.

Solitary or phaceloid, separate corallites sometimes joined by thin encrustations of peritheca. Average height of corallite 5 to 6 mm, diameter 5 mm. Low, flat, equal costae, densely granulate, distinct down to base of corallite. Four cycles of septa, fourth incomplete, first and second reach columella, third bend in to join second, and fourth bend and fuse with third. None of septa very exsert, all denticulate, less marked in first and second cycles. Columella weak and spongy.

39. *Astrangia rathbuni* Vaughan.

Similar to *A. solitaria* but inner edges of septa slope more gradually to the floor of cup, which is shallower. Not a true reef coral.

40. *Astrangia brasiliensis* Vaughan.

See Proc. U.S. Nat. Museum (1906), 30:848.

Cups more widely separated than the other two species and encrusting base thinner. Not a true reef coral.

41. *Phyllangia americana* Edwards and Haime.

Encrusting, consisting of moderately large cups 10 mm in diameter, nearly circular and deep at center. Septa usually pronged beyond wall of cup. Cups deeper than in *Astrangia* and columella more rudimentary. Not a true reef coral.

42. *Oculina diffusa* Lamarck, (Plate 34).

Described by Verrill (1902), page 175.

Consists of close bushy branches bearing shallow cups, each about 3.5 mm across. Branches usually less than 10 mm thick. Very abundant, Florida, Bermuda, the Bahamas, and the West Indies. Not found off Brazil.

Forms densely ramose colony by alternate extratentacular building, no axial corallite. Calices 3 to 4 mm in diameter, sometimes circumvallate, septa usually 24, rather narrow, slightly exsert. Well-developed columella.

43. *Oculina valenciennesi* Edwards and Haime.

Described by Verrill (1902), page 176.

Larger and more straggling compared to *O. diffusa.* Cups slightly sunken with groove surrounding them, slightly larger than *O. diffusa.* Found in Bermuda and the West Indies, not so far in Florida.

Branches more open and irregular than *O. diffusa,* often over 1 foot high. Larger branches 12 to 20 mm in diameter in large specimens. Corallites usually circumvallate, low and scarcely exsert. Curved costal striations cross circumvalleys. Calices average 4 mm ranging from 3 to 5 mm in diameter.

44. *Oculina varicosa* Lesueur.

Described by Verrill (1902), page 173.

The largest of the ivory corals, up to 2 feet high. Branches fewer and longer than *O. diffusa* and *O. valenciennesi,* and main part much wider. Cups swollen at base, except on smaller branches, with bottom 10 mm or more across, and top 3.5 mm. Comparatively rare, found in Bermuda and occasionally on the Florida reef and in the West Indies.

Branching irregular, arborescent, main trunk up to 50 mm, branches long, crooked, and tapering. Corallites mammiform, bases less swollen at tips of branches. Costal striae well developed, about 24, sometimes lacking on larger branches. Septa 24 to 36, rarely more in large corallites. Calices 2.75 to 3.50 mm in diameter, rarely 4 mm, bases of corallites up to 12 mm wide and 8 mm high.

45. *Meandrina meandrites* (Linnaeus), (Plate 35).

Also *Pectinia meandrites,* (Matthai 1928).

Described by Matthai (1928), pages 161-166.

Forms large boulders, flat or rounded, up to over 1 foot. Valleys long and twisting but not all interconnected, about 10 mm wide, 8 mm deep. Wall occasionally has groove about 2 mm wide and about 4 mm deep. Septa of adjacent valleys usually meet in sharp zigzag line on top of separating wall. About 7 larger septa per cm, over 1 mm thick, no teeth on margins, with smaller septa alternating. Found in Florida and the West Indies.

Massive, heavy, flat, convex, or irregular. Discontinuous valleys, long and sinuous, 8 to 14 mm wide, average 11 mm, 6 to 10 mm deep, average 8 mm. Rarely short valleys. Colline, occasionally with groove up to 4 mm wide, average depth 1.5 mm, up to 5 mm, rarely discontinuous. Septa of adjacent valleys usually meet in a sharp zigzag line on top of colline. Principal septa 6.8 per cm, 1.2 mm thick, 4.5 mm deep. Margins of septa vertical, entire with granules on sides. Smaller narrow septa alternate. Septa exsert 1 to 1.5 mm, exsert ends arched. Columella lamellar, sometimes of twisted solid trabeculae or two or three parallel lamellae, continuous. Sometimes rudimentary or discontinuous.

46. *Meandrina brasiliensis* (Edwards and Haime).

Also *Pectinia brasiliensis,* (Matthai 1928).

Described by Matthai (1928), pages 167-169.

Smaller than *M. meandrites.* Flat or rounded on top, conical below with short stalk. Valleys interconnect usually with side valleys opening off a single, lengthwise central valley. Otherwise similar to *M. meandrites.* Not very common. Brazil, Florida reefs, and the West Indies.

Turbinate, somewhat convex, short penduncle. Continuous valley with midlongtitudinal and paired lateral lobes as in *Manicina areolata,* width 15 to 20 mm. Colline somewhat thickened with groove about 2 mm wide, or ridged, about 2 mm thick.

47. *Meandrina danae* (Edwards and Haime).

Described as *Pectinia danae* by Vaughan (1902), page 297. He believes it to be a form of *M. brasiliensis.* It differs in having a blister-like coating on the surface outside of the cups. This hides the extensions of the septa.

48. *Dichocoenia stokesii,* Edwards and Haime, (Plate 37).

Described by Matthai (1928), pages 198-201.

Forms heavy boulders up to one foot in diameter. Short valleys, separate from each other, walls projecting from general surface. Septa thick, without teeth. Found on Florida reefs, in the Bahamas, and in the West Indies.

Convex or rounded, heavy. Narrow, short discontinuous valleys. Mono-, di-, and tri-stomodoeal polyps. Intramural budding. Valleys slightly curved, up to 28 mm long, 3 to 5 mm wide, 4 to 5 mm deep, lateral branches or terminal forks rare. Walls vary in amount of projection, up to 7 mm. Walls 1 to 1.5 mm thick, and up to 5 mm apart toward edge of corallum. Peritheca granular or vesicular. Septa alternately thick and thin, about 10 of each per cm. Thick septa about 0.75 mm toward wall. Five to 8 thin septa and all thick septa meet columella. Thick septa exsert to 1 mm, lower broadened parts sometimes form paliform lobes. Columella of closely twisted trabeculae, 1 mm broad. Costae correspond to septa, but thicker, with granular edges.

49. *Dendrogyra cylindrus* Ehrenberg, (Plates 38, 39).

Described by Matthai (1928), page 170.

Forms heavy pillars up to 2 feet long, wide at base. Winding, narrow valleys, not all interconnected. Thick septa without teeth. Narrow walls between valleys. Found on the Florida reefs, in the Bahamas, and in the West Indies.

Heavy, massive, rising into cylindrical branches which may reach 60 cm in length, with a broad base up to 20 cm in diameter. Sinuous, discontinuous valleys, often short, 3 to 4 mm wide, 2.5 mm deep. Collines average 3 mm thick, up to 5 mm, usually with shallow groove. Septa nondentate, sides granular, alternately thick and thin, 7 to 10 per cm. Thick septa, 1 mm thick, meet columella, exsert up to 1.25 mm. Exsert portion arched with sharp margin, terminating at edge of groove. Columella solid, 1 mm thick, centers not marked. Sometimes reduced columella and septa, meeting across valley.

50. *Mussismilia brasiliensis* (Verrill).

Also *Protomussa brasiliensis,* (Matthai 1928), also *Mussa (Symphyllia) brasiliensis,* and *Mussa (Symphyllia) tenuisepta,* (Verrill 1902).

Described by Matthai (1928), page 269.

Cups up to 25 mm long, irregularly oval, separated by grooves. Septa with teeth not directed upward as in *Mussa*. Found only on the Brazilian reefs.

Massive and heavy, calicinal surface convex, lower surface with broad attachment. Mono-, di-, and tri-stomodoeal polyps. Corallites 12 to 15 mm wide, up to 25 mm long, 7 mm deep, narrowing toward columella. Collines 3 to 6 mm, with groove above. Septa 10 to 12 per cm, six principals, continuing over colline or meeting in groove, principals about .75 mm thick, exsert about 1 mm. Septa perforated, teeth coarse, directed horizontally. Columella well developed, 2 to 3 mm in width of closely twisted septal trabeculae.

51. *Mussismilia harttii* (Verrill).

Also *Protomussa harttii,* (Matthai 1928), also *Mussa harttii,* (Verrill 1902).

Described by Matthai (1928), page 270.

Cups irregular in shape, from 12 to 30 mm across, on ends of branches which are joined together along a varying part of their length. Similar in other respects to *M. brasiliensis,* but septal teeth thinner. Found only in Brazil.

Branching, branches dividing dichotomously, peritheca present or absent in varying quantity so that branches vary in degree of separation. Corallites up to 30 mm long, 12 to 15 mm wide and about 10 mm deep. Walls sharply ridged, about 2 mm thick. Septa with many irregular teeth, thinner than *M. brasiliensis,* about 12 to 14 per cm, about six principal, up to 1.5 mm exsert. Columella of twisted septal trabeculae, well developed, 2 to 2.5 mm wide. Costae traverse greater length of corallites with slender teeth directed upward.

52. *Mussa angulosa* (Pallas), (Plates 41, 42).

Also *Mussa lacera* (Pallas) Oken, (Verrill 1902).

Described by Matthai (1928), pages 104-108.

Heavy, short branches ending in cups up to 12 cm long and 4.5 wide. Walls 6 to 8 mm thick. Septa have strong teeth pointing obliquely upward. Toothed ridges continuous with the costae run lengthwise down branches. Found in the Bahamas and the West Indies, more rarely off the Florida Keys.

Branches divergent, heavy, large, calices forming convex upper surface. Valleys often constricted between columellar centers. Up to 12 cm long and 4.5 cm wide, down to 2 cm width between centers. Walls 6 to 8 mm thick, often angular. Septa 8 per cm, four or five principals sloping to meet columella. Septal margins with about nine large blunt teeth, directed obliquely upward, upper ones 4 mm long and 3 mm wide at base, sides spinulose. Septa exsert up to 6 mm, with two teeth on exsert portion. Columella well developed, centers 4 to 5 mm in width, made of thin interlaced trabeculae. Costae continuous with septa extending down wall, with upward directed teeth.

53. *Scolymia lacera* (Pallas).

Discussed by Wells (1964), page 381.

This was thought to be a young stage of *Mussa angulosa.* However, it always consists of large, circular, solitary cups up to 6 cm in diameter, has a single center to the valley, and is not branched. Radiating septa have large teeth and extend beyond wall of cup. Usually in deeper water.

54. *Isophyllastrea rigida* (Dana), (Plate 43).

Also *Mussa (Symphyllia) rigida* (Dana), (Verrill 1902).
Described by Matthai (1928), pages 263-268.

Small boulders. Cups polygonal and irregular in shape. Septa have six to eight large teeth on their edges and extend over the walls. Wall about 3 mm thick, cups about 10 mm across, but may be much longer. Found in the West Indies, Bahamas, Bermuda, and the Florida Keys.

Hemispherical, small, evenly convex, with broad attachment on lower surface. Cerioid. Calices tend to be polygonal. Mono-, and di-stomodoeal. Monostomodoeal calices 10 to 12 mm deep. Collines 2 to 4 mm thick with faint groove or ridge on upper surface. Twenty-five to 30 septa in single corallites, five to eight meeting the columella, thicker (1 to 1.5 mm) toward wall, narrow, and almost vertical edge. Margins with six to eight coarse teeth, lower ones larger, directed obliquely upward. Sides of septa rough. Septa meet in groove or continuous over ridge, exsert to 1.5 mm, exsert portion toothed. Columella feeble, of loosely interlocking trabeculae.

55. *Mycetophyllia lamarckiana* (Edwards and Haime), (Plates 44, 45).

Described by Matthai (1928), pages 250, 255.

Forms rather flat growths, either stalked or completely encrusting on old rock. Chocolate ground color, but frequently overlaid with bright green. Valleys interconnected and walls tend to disappear in older corals. Septa toothed. Two or three parallel vertical toothed strips run lengthwise in the valleys.

Subturbinate or encrusting, pedicelled or not. Valley continuous, sinuous. Colline disappears partly in older coralla. Valley 12 to 15 mm wide, about 10 mm deep. Colline 2 to 3 mm thick, sometimes up to 5 mm, ridged or slightly grooved. Septa 8 to 10 per cm, four or five extending further into valley. Larger ones with seven to nine teeth, directed obliquely upward. Slightly exsert, exsert ends toothed. Continuous over colline. Sides sometimes rough. Columella absent but septa converge toward centers, which are connected by two or three toothed lamellae. Thin epitheca covers under surface to within 10 mm of edge.

56. *Isophyllia sinuosa* (Ellis and Solander), (Plate 46).

Also *Isophyllia fragilis* (Dana), and *Isophyllia dispsacea* (Dana), (Verrill 1902).

Described by Matthai (1928), pages 237-247.

Color variegated with patches of lavender, bright green and white. Frequently bright green is predominant in the Florida Keys.

Medium size, massive, with short stalk, up to 6 or 8 inches. Valley continuous, lobes radiating from center, average width 22 mm widening toward rim, up to 35 mm, depth 8 to 10 mm. Valley becomes discontinuous in older colonies, losing radial arrangement. Circumscribed corallites possess one or two columellar centers. Colline usually ridged, sometimes with shallow groove above, swollen at base, 3 to 8 mm. Septa 7 to 9 per cm, four or five principal, very sloping margins which have six to 10 slender coarse teeth, lower ones larger, directed obliquely upward, sides spinulose. Septa thicker toward columella, usually 2 mm. Principals exsert to 5 mm at edge of corallum, elsewhere 2 mm. Septa continuous over colline or meet in groove, extending to pedicel. Thin epitheca over noncalicinal surface except within 10 mm of edge. Variety *dispsacea* more spinous and lighter corallum, collines and septa thinner, hence appearing less crowded. Calices deeper and steeper.

57. *Isophyllia multiflora* Verrill, (Plate 47).

Also *Mussa (Symphyllia) annectens*, (Verrill 1902).

Described by Matthai (1928), page 248.

Similar in most respects to *I. sinuosa*, but greener in color, smaller, more singular cups, fewer and narrower valleys, walls thinner, septa more crowded, thinner, and less protruding.

Smaller than *I. sinuosa*. Valleys shorter and narrower, average 14 mm wide up to 20 mm, less open. Colline thinner. Septa to 12 per cm, four or five principal, thinner, less exsert. Columella less developed. Of loosely interlocked septal trabeculae.

58. *Eusmilia fastigiata* (Pallas), (Plate 48).

Also *Eusmilia aspera* (Dana), (Verrill 1902).

Described by Matthai (1928), page 190.

Branched with cups at ends of branches. More or less oval, up to 35 mm long, with sharp rim. No teeth to septa. Small toothed ridges extend from septa down outer part of cup and branch. Deep brown in color with greenish cup ringed with whitish tentacles. Florida, Bahamas, and the West Indies.

Branching, Corallites with mono- to tri-stomodoeal polyps, often triangular. Valley up to 35 mm long. 8 to 13 mm wide, 8 mm deep. Wall 2 mm thick with sharp rim. Septa 15 to 18 per cm, seven to nine principals, 3.5 to 4 mm broad, thickening to 2 mm at wall, exsert to 2.5 mm. Subsidiaries thinner and less exsert. Margins entire sides with granular triae. Columella of closely twisted trabeculae, 1 mm broad, sharp above with wavy, often continuous ridge. Costae extend greater length of branches, irregularly toothed.

59. *Tubastrea tenuilamellosa* (Edwards and Haime).

Boschma (1953) gives an exhaustive description of this species. Also in Verrill (1867-71) as *Dendrophyllia*, page 508.

Low rounded convex clumps up to 6 cm diameter with tubular cups projecting about 1 cm from spongy encrusting base. Walls, septa porous, continue as ridges on outer wall of cup. Four cycles, rarely five. Columella well developed, occupies about one-third of width of cup, of contorted porous plates. Color of living coral bright orange. Not a true reef coral.

60. *Millepora alcicornis Linnaeus.*

The "stinging coral" is not a true coral, but is included here on account of its superficial similarity and its extensive distribution throughout the whole of the western Atlantic coral reef area. The general form varies from an encrusting growth over dead sea whips or shells, to a branching structure, which may grow out from the encrustation. The branches may resemble the staghorn coral, *Acropora palmata* in miniature. Sometimes a flattened frond-like or hand-like growth takes place. The entire surface is covered with minute holes, barely visible to the naked eye, arranged in numerous groups of five smaller ones around a central larger one. Through these holes project the small polyps. The larger gastrozooids or feeding polyps project through the larger holes and the slimmer club-ended dactylozooids or stinging polyps arise from the smaller holes. The color varies from light orange-yellow to dark brown.

Glossary of Principal Technical Terms in Coral Taxonomy

basal plate: The lower part of the coral cup, separating the polyp from the substrate.

calice: The upper or open end of the corallite or coral cup.

centers: Regions in a series which correspond to the centers of calices.

cerioid: Form of colony when corallites or individual coral cups are closely pressed together and directly united by their walls, resulting in polygonal cups or calices.

coenenchyme: Coral skeleton formed outside the wall of the cup or corallite.

coenosarc: The soft part of the polyp which lies against the outside of the coral wall or cup.

columella: Central axial structure formed from inner ends of septa.

compound: Used to describe trabeculae composed of a series of bundles of sclerodermites or centers of calcification.

corallite: The coral structure or cup formed by an individual polyp in the colony.

corallum: The entire coral formed by a colony.

costae: Continuations of the septa beyond the wall or theca.

dendroid: With spreading branches, each a single corallite.

dissepiment: Horizontal plates between septa or costae cutting off older, lower, parts of skeleton and supporting the polyp.

edge-zone: Part of the polyp which extends beyond the wall of the cup over the general coral surface.

encrusting: Coral growth which forms thin, continuous sheets directly attached to the substrate.

endotheca: Consists of intrathecal dissepiments or horizontal plates within the cup or coral wall.

epitheca: The vertical coral wall rising from the basal plate.

essential: A columella similar in origin to pali. May be a group of twisted rods or fused into a single style.

exothecal: Extrathecal dissepiments or horizontal plates outside the cup or coral wall.

exsert: Margins of septa higher than the theca or coral cup.

extratentacular: When buds are formed from the edge zone or the soft part lying outside the ring of tentacles.

fan system: Arrangement of trabeculae inclined outward from an axis of divergence. Several fan systems may exist in one septum.

fenestrate: Septum of loosely connected trabeculae with pores of perforations between trabeculae.

flabelloid: Meandroid corals with a single linear series or row of polyps.

foliaceous: Branching in thin expanded sheets.

fossa: Central cavity of a corallite or cup.

granulations: Where sclerodermites or centers of calcification inclining outward emerge at the surface of a septum.

hydnophoroid: Corallite centers arranged around conical hillocks.

intratentacular budding: Buds formed from that part of the polyp surrounding the mouth and ringed by the tentacles.

lamellar: Columella is a vertical plate, free above, lying lengthwise in the long axis of the elongated corallite.

laminar: Septum formed of trabeculae closely united to form a continuous sheet.

massive: Forming thick masses.

meandroid: Corallites forming groups or series within common walls, so as to form valleys.

oral disc: That part of the coral polyp surrounding the mouth and ringed by the tentacles.

pali: Inner ends of septa, separated.

paratheca: Wall formed from dissepiments.

parietal: Columella formed by intermingling of trabeculae from inner margin of septa.

peritheca: Extrathecal skeleton deposited by coenosarc.

phaceloid: Parallel branches forming clumps or tufts.

plocoid: Corallites united by peritheca and not directly by their walls.

ramose: Branching colonies.

reptoid: Budding from stolon-like expansions of edge zone.

sclerodermites: Primary units of skeleton. Centers of calcification with their fascicles of fibers. Epitheca, basal plates, and dissepiments lack these. They are present in septa and related structures only.

septa: Radiating vertical plates.

septotheca: Formed by thickenings of outer parts of septa.

series: A group of corallites within a common wall.

simple: A trabeculum composed of a series of single sclerodermites.

stereome: Layer of secondary thickening of septa or related parts.

synapticulae: Rods joining adjacent septa.

synapticulotheca: Similar to septotheca but not solid. Formed from synapticulae.

thamnasteroid: Without definite boundaries and with confluent septa.

theca: Wall uniting outer edges of septa.

trabecula: A vertical series of sclerodermites or centers of calcification.

turbinate: Inverted cone or top-shaped.

Taxonomic Key to Genera of Living Western Atlantic Corals

(Numbers leading only to ahermatypic corals are in parentheses)

1. Septa laminar or rudimentary consisting of relatively few simple (rarely compound) trabeculae, strongly inclined from axis of divergence. Suborder ASTROCOENIIDA. 2
   Septa laminar or fenestrate, well developed, consisting of numerous simple or compound trabeculae slightly inclined from the axis of divergence 5
2. Peritheca almost invariably absent. Septal margins beaded. Family Astrocoeniidae 3
   Peritheca extensively developed 4
3. Septal margins with well-marked dentations. Corallum cerioid . . . . *Astrocoenia*
   Septal margins smooth or minutely dentate. Corallum plocoid . . . . *Stephanocoenia*
4. Peritheca nonporous, solid, or vesicular. Family Seriatoporidae . . . . *Madracis*
   Peritheca porous, ventriculate. Family Acroporidae *Acropora*
5. Septa consist of one or more fan systems of simple or compound trabeculae, porous or solid, margins beaded or dentate 6

	Septa consist of one fan system of mostly simple trabeculae. Margins mostly smooth	29
6.	Septa fenestrate composed of simple trabeculae, but often appearing laminar in later stages, more or less porous, margins beaded; simple synapticulae present. Suborder FUNGIIDA	7
	Septa laminar, nonporous, margins dentate, sometimes minutely; synapticulae absent. Suborder FAVIIDA	9
7.	Septa fenestrate in young stages and higher cycles, laminar in later stages. Superfamily Agariciidae	8
	Septa fenestrate and porous in all stages. Family Poritidae	*Porites*
8.	Wall septothecal in ephebic stage, sometimes reduced or absent. Septa of simple trabeculae, laminar. Family Agariciidae	*Agaricia*
	Wall synapticulothecal. Fenestrate structure marked (less so in later stages). Septa of simple and compound trabeculae, more or less porous. Family Siderastreidae.	*Siderastrea*
9.	Septa consist of one or two fan systems of trabeculae. Septal teeth never very large and coarse	10
	Septa of more than two fan systems of trabeculae. Septal dentations large and coarse. Family Mussidae . .	25
10.	Septal trabeculae simple or compound. Margins strongly dentate	11
	Septal trabeculae simple, in one fan system. Margins minutely dentate	21
11.	Septal dentations regular. Family Faviidae	12
	Septal dentations irregular. Reptoid budding. (Family Astrangiidae)	(18)
12.	Intratentacular budding. No directive mesenteries except in young polyps. Subfamily Faviinae	13
	Extratentacular budding. Directive mesenteries in all polyps. Subfamily Montastreinae	16

13. Colonies plocoid, corallites united nearly to tops by peritheca. Costate . . . . *Favia*
    Colonies meandroid, series sinuous, usually long 14
14. Septa lack internal lobes. Trabecular linkages between centers . . . . *Diploria*
    The larger septa with internal lobes, which are small and narrow. Linkages trabecular or lamellar 15
15. Trabecular linkage, walls mostly parathecal, valleys broad . . . . *Manicina*
    Lamellar linkage . . . . *Colpophyllia*
16. Phaceloid, paliform lobes, papillose columella present. Exotheca not vesicular . . . . *Cladocora*
    Plocoid, parietal spongy columella, vesicular exotheca. 17
17. Peritheca costate, exotheca vesicular, septal margin regularly dentate . . . . *Montastrea*
    Peritheca almost without costae, very vesicular, appearing blistered . . . . *Solenastrea*

(18) Colonies reptoid. Septa of first two or three cycles obscurely dentate and exert . . . . (19)
    Colonies plocoid, united basally by peritheca . . . . (20)

(19) Corallites united by thin stolon-like expansions. Columella papillary . . . . (*Oulangia*)
    Corallites united by some peritheca. Columella feeble . . . . (*Phyllangia*)

(20) Columella papillose or spongy. All septa dentate (*Astrangia*)
    Columella appears lamellar. Only lower cycles of septa obscurely dentate (*Colangia*)

21. Dendroid. Extratentacular budding; peritheca dense, solid. Endotheca subtabular. Family Oculinidae 22
    Meandroid. Intratentacular budding. Peritheca dense, if developed. Endotheca vesicular. Family Trochosmiliidae 23
22. Columella parietal, feeble. Corallites filling with stereome. No pali . . . . *Madrepora*

Columella of twisted trabecular processes, well developed. Pali in irregular crown before first one or two cycles. Axial corallite absent. . . . . *Oculina*

23. Peritheca absent, columella lamellar, if developed. Subfamily Meandrininae . . . . *Meandrina*
    Peritheca dense, columella parietal. Subfamily Dichocoeniinae 24
24. Corallite series mono- to tricentric and short, united by peritheca . . . . *Dichocoenia*
    Corallite series long, united directly by septothecal walls. . . . . *Dendrogyra*
25. Solitary . . . . *Scolymia*
    Phaceloid colonies 26
    Cerioid or meandroid 27
26. Septal dentations lacerate and irregular . . . . *Mussismilia*
    Septal dentations regular . . . . *Mussa*
27. Cerioid, mono- to tricentric. Feeble columella *Isophyllastrea*
    Meandroid 28
28. Series long, lamellar linkage, collines discontinuous, enclosing several series. No columella. . . . . . *Mycetophyllia*
    Series short, trabecular linkage. . . . . *Isophyllia*
29. Septa always laminar and nonporous, margins smooth, no synapticulae. Suborder CARYOPHYLLIIDA 30
    Septa secondary thickened singularly porous, margins smooth or beaded. Synapticulae present. (Suborder DENDROPHYLIIDA) . . . . (56)
30. Corallite wall septothecal. Superfamily Caryophyllioidae. Corallite wall epithecal. (Superfamily Flabelloidae) . . . . (54)
31. Wall imperforate. Family Caryophylliidae 32
    Wall often perforate when first formed. (Family Guyniidae) . . . . (52)
32. Endotheca absent . . . . (33)
    Endotheca present 44

(33) Corallum not entirely covered by the polyp. (Subfamily Caryophylliinae) . . . . (34)
Corallum entirely covered by the polyp. (Subfamily Turboliniidae) . . . . (43)
(34) Pali or paliform lobes present . . . . (35)
Pali absent . . . . (40)
(35) Pali in one crown before third cycle . . . . (36)
Paliform lobes, irregular, before third cycle. *(Bathycyathus)*
Pali in two crowns before all but last cycle . . . . (37)
Pali in several crowns, indistinct, before all but last cycle, solitary, turbinate to trochoid . . . . *(Paracyathus)*
(36) Solitary . . . . *(Caryophyllia)*
Colonial, small phaceloid colony. . . . . *(Coenocyathus)*
(37) Pali simple . . . . (38)
Pali of one crown unite in deltas. Corallum discoidal. *(Deltocyathus)*
(38) Corallum turbinate to ceratoid . . . . (39)
Corallum globular or bottle-shaped . . . . . *(Peponocyathus)*
(39) Epitheca absent . . . . *(Trochocyathus)*
Epitheca present . . . . *(Tethocyathus)*
(40) Columella absent . . . . (41)
Columella fascicular . . . . (42)
Columella axially elongate with secondary thickened lamellar elements. . . . . *(Oxysmilia)*
(41) Patellate . . . . *(Stephanocyathus)*
Turbinate . . . . *(Vaughanelia)*
(42) Columella crispate at surface . . . . *(Cyathoceras)*
Columella papillose . . . . *(Ceratotrochus)*
(43) Columella parietal, pali present . . . . *(Paradeltocyathus)*
Columella styliform, corallum trochoid. . . . . . *(Turbinolia)*
Columella lamellar appearance . . . . *(Sphenotrochus)*
44. Endotheca sparse and deep. (Subfamily Desmophylliidea) . . . . (45)
Endotheca well developed 46
(45) Solitary . . . . *(Desmophyllum)*

	Dendroid	*(Lophelia)*
46.	Mostly solitary. Colonies dendroid. Extratentacular budding. (Subfamily Parasmiliinae)	(47)
	Colonial. Phaceloid. Intratentacular budding. Subfamily Eusmiliinae	*Eusmilia*
(47)	Paliform lobes absent	(48)
	Paliform lobes present	(51)
(48)	Columella feeble or absent	(49)
	Columella spongy	*(Parasmilia)*
(49)	Solitary	*(Dungulia)*
	Colonial	(50)
(50)	Subdendroid. Mature polyps not continuous	*(Anomocora)*
	Dendroid or phaceloid	*(Solenosmilia)*
(51)	Paliform lobes before third cycle	*(Caryosmilia)*
	Lobes before all but last cycle	*(Asterosmilia)*
(52)	Columella absent	*(Schizocyathus)*
	Columella present	(53)
(53)	Pali absent	*(Guynia)*
	Pali in one crown of six	*(Stenocyathus)*
(54)	Columella feeble or absent	(55)
	Columella pareital. Corallum turbinate-trochoid	*(Gardineria)*
(55)	Corallum cuneiform or compressed turbinate. No basal rootlets	*(Flabellum)*
	Basal rootlets developed	*(Monomyces)*
(56)	Septa normal in ephebic stage	(57)
	Septa according to Pourtales plan in ephebic stage	(61)
(57)	Solitary	(58)
	Colonial	(60)
(58)	Costae distinct	*(Trochopsammia)*
	Costae replaced by spines	(59)
(59)	Columella feeble	*(Thecopsammia)*
	Columella well developed	*(Bathypsammia)*
(60)	Corallum dendroid	*(Enallopsammia)*
	Corallum plocoid	*(Tubastrea)*
(61)	Solitary	*(Balanophyllia)*
	Colonial, dendroid	*(Dendrophyllia)*

Selected Bibliography

This list is primarily selected for additional reading for those who are not serious students of the systematics of corals or the geology of coral reefs. Graduate students will find more extensive and technical sources of information in the literature cited in the more recent of the works included here.

Coral Reefs in General

Roughley, T. C. 1947. Wonders of the Great Barrier Reef. Charles Scribner's Sons, New York. Nontechnical and very well illustrated.

Wells, J. W. 1957. Coral reefs, pp. 609-631. *In* Treatise on marine ecology and paleontology, ed. by Joel Hedgpeth. Vol. I, Geological Society of America Memoirs 67.

Yonge, C. M. 1930. A year on the Great Barrier Reef. G. P. Putnam's Sons, New York. Nontechnical but authoritative. Deals with the Great Barrier Reef expedition.

Formation of Coral Reefs

Davis, W. M. 1928. The coral reef problem. American Geographical Society Special Publication 9. The most complete account available of the origin of coral reefs.

Emery, Kenneth O., J. I. Tracey, and H. S. Ladd. 1949. Submarine geology and topography in the northern Marshalls. American Geophysical Union Transaction 30 (1).

Emery, Kenneth O., J. I. Tracey, and H. S. Ladd. 1954. Geology of Bikini and nearby atolls. U.S. Geological Survey Professional Paper, 266-A.

Emiliani, C. 1966. Palaeotemperature analysis of Caribbean cores. Journal of Geology 76 (2), 109-126.

Hess, H. H. 1946. Drowned ancient islands of the Pacific basin. American Journal of Science 244.

Hess, H. H. 1948. Drowned ancient islands of the Pacific basin. Smithsonian Report for 1947, Washington, D.C.

Hoffmeister, J. E. and H. G. Multer. 1968. Geology and origin of the Florida Keys. Geological Society of American Bulletin 79, 1487-1502.

Kuenen, P. H. 1947. Two problems of marine geology: atolls and canyons. Verhandelingen der Koninklijke Nederlandsche Akademie van Wetenschappen, Afd. Natuurkunde, Tweede Sectie. Deel XLIII (3).

Ladd, H. S. and J. I. Tracey, Jr. 1949. The problem of coral reefs. Scientific Monthly 69 (5).

Mesolella, K. J., R. K. Matthews, Wallace S. Broecker, and David L. Thurber. 1969. The astronomical theory of climatic change: Barbados data. Journal of Geology 27 (3).

Moore, Raymond C., ed. 1956. Treatise of invertebrate paleontology, Part F, Coelenterata. Geological Society of America and University of Kansas Press, Lawrence, Kansas.

Sayles, Robert W. 1931. Bermuda during the ice age. Proceedings of the American Academy of Arts and Sciences 66 (9).

Schuchert, Charles. 1935. Historical geology of the Antillean-Caribbean region. John Wiley & Sons Inc., New York. Deals with the geology of the Caribbean reefs.

Vaughan, T. W. 1919. Fossil corals from Central America, Cuba, and Porto Rico with an account of the American Tertiary, Pleistocene, and Recent reefs. U.S. National Museum Bulletin 103.

Wiens, Harold J. 1962. Atoll environment and ecology. Yale University Press, New Haven, Conn.

Structure and Habits of Living Corals

Vaughan, T. W. 1916. Results of investigations of the ecology of the Floridian and Bahamian shoal-water corals. National Academy of Science Proceedings 2, 95-100. A useful summary of Dr. Vaughan's publications on this subject. Other papers are to be found in the Year Books 9-14 of the Carnegie Institution, Washington, D.C.

Vaughan, T. W. and J. W. Wells. 1943. Revision of the Scleractinia. Geological Society of America, Special Papers 44. This study summarizes present-day knowledge of structure and ecology and is the most up-to-date taxonomic revision. A classified bibliography is included. A valuable handbook for the student of corals.

Yonge, C. M. 1930. A year on the Great Barrier Reef. G. P. Putnam's Sons, New York.

Associates of Living Corals

Abbott, R. Tucker. 1954. American seashells. D. Van Nostrand Co., Inc., New York.

Bartsch. P. 1937. An ecological cross section of the lower part of Florida. Report of the Committee on Paleoecology. National Research Council, Washington, D.C.

Roughley, T. C. 1947. Wonders of the Great Barrier Reef. Charles Scribner's Sons, New York.

Russell, F. S. and C. M. Yonge. 1944. The seas. Frederick Warne & Co., Inc., New York.

Smith, Maxwell. 1945. East coast marine shells. Edwards Brothers, Ann Arbor, Mich.

Warmke, G. and R. T. Abbott. 1962. Caribbean seashells. Livingston Publishers, Narberth, Pa.

Yonge, C. M. 1930. A year on the Great Barrier Reef. G. P. Putnam's Sons, New York.

The Atlantic Corals

Beschma, H. 1953. On specimens of the coral genus *Tubastraea,* with notes on phenomena of fission. Studies Fauna Curaçao 4 (18).

Goreau, T. 1959. The ecology of Jamaican coral reefs. Ecology 40 (1), 67-90.

Goreau, T. F. and J. W. Wells. 1967. The shallow-water Scleractinia of Jamaica. Bulletin of Marine Science 17 (2), 442-453. Revised list of species and vertical range. Gives additional bibliography on Jamaican reefs.

Matthai, G. 1928. A monograph of the recent Meandroid Astreidae. Catalogue of Madreporaria. British Museum 7.

Pourtales, L. F. de. 1870. Florida reef corals. Mem. Museum of Comparative Zoology, Harvard II.

Rathbun, R. 1879. Brazilian corals and coral reefs. American Naturalist XIII, 539-551.

Roos, P. J. 1964. The distribution of reef corals in Curaçao. Studies Fauna Curaçao 20 (81).

Squires, D. F. 1963. Neotropica 9 (28).

Vaughan, T. W. 1901. Stony corals of the Porto Rican waters. U.S. Fish Commission, Bulletin for 1900. Part 2, pp. 289-320.

Vaughan, T. W. 1919. Fossil corals from Central America, Cuba, and Porto Rico with an account of the American Tertiary, Pleistocene, and Recent reefs. U.S. National Museum Bulletin 103.

Verrill, A. E. 1902. Papers on corals. *In* Transactions, Connecticut Academy of Arts and Sciences XI, 63-266.

Wells, J. W. 1964. The Recent solitary mussid scleractinian corals. Zool. Meded. 39.

Additional Sources

Milliman, J. D. 1965. An annotated bibliography of recent papers on corals and coral reefs. Atoll Research Bulletin III. Pacific Science Board, National Academy of Sciences, National Research Council.

Pugh, W. E. (Ed.). 1950. Bibliography of organic reef bioderms and biostomes. Seismograph Service Corporation, Tulsa, Okla.

Ranson, Gilbert. 1958. Coraux et récifs corallieux. Bullétin de L'Institut Océanographique (Monaco) 55 (1121).

Vaughan, T. W. and J. W. Wells. 1943. Revision of the Scleractinia. Geological Society of America. Special Papers 44. Gives bibliography of over 1000 titles.

Plates

1. Surface of *Madracis decactis* (Lyman) x 14 1/3 *M.L. 8.102

*M.L. numbers refer to specimens in the marine biological reference collection of the Rosenstiel School of Marine and Atmospheric Science, University of Miami.

2. Surface of *Stephanocoenia michelini* Edwards and Haime x 20

3. Portion of branch of *Acropora cervicornis* (Lamarck) x 4/5
M.L. 8.6

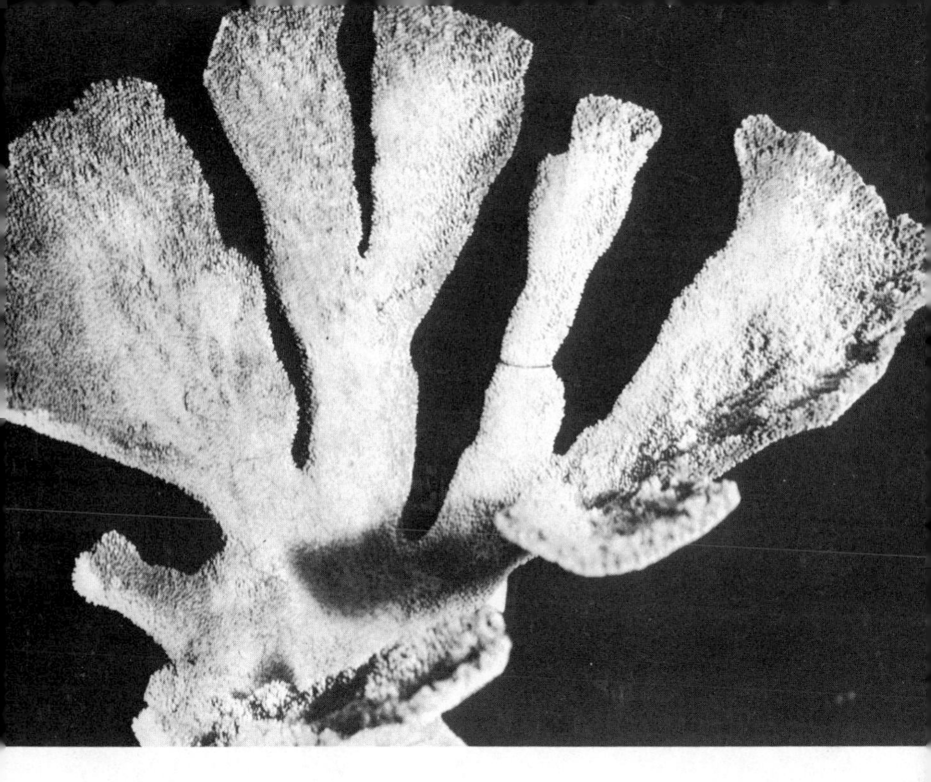

4. Portion of branch of *Acropora palmata* (Lamarck) x 1/4
M.L. 8.1

5. Colony of *Agaricia agaricites* (Linnaeus) x 4/5 M.L. 8.16

6. Surface of *Agaricia agaricites* (Linnaeus) x 4 4/5 M.L. 8.149

7. Colony of *Agaricia nobilis* Verrill x 3

8. Colony of *Agaricia fragilis* Dana x 3/4

9. Surface of *Siderastrea radians* (Pallas) x 15 1/3 M.L. 8.22

10. Surface of *Siderastrea siderea* (Ellis and Solander) x 11
M.L. 8.21

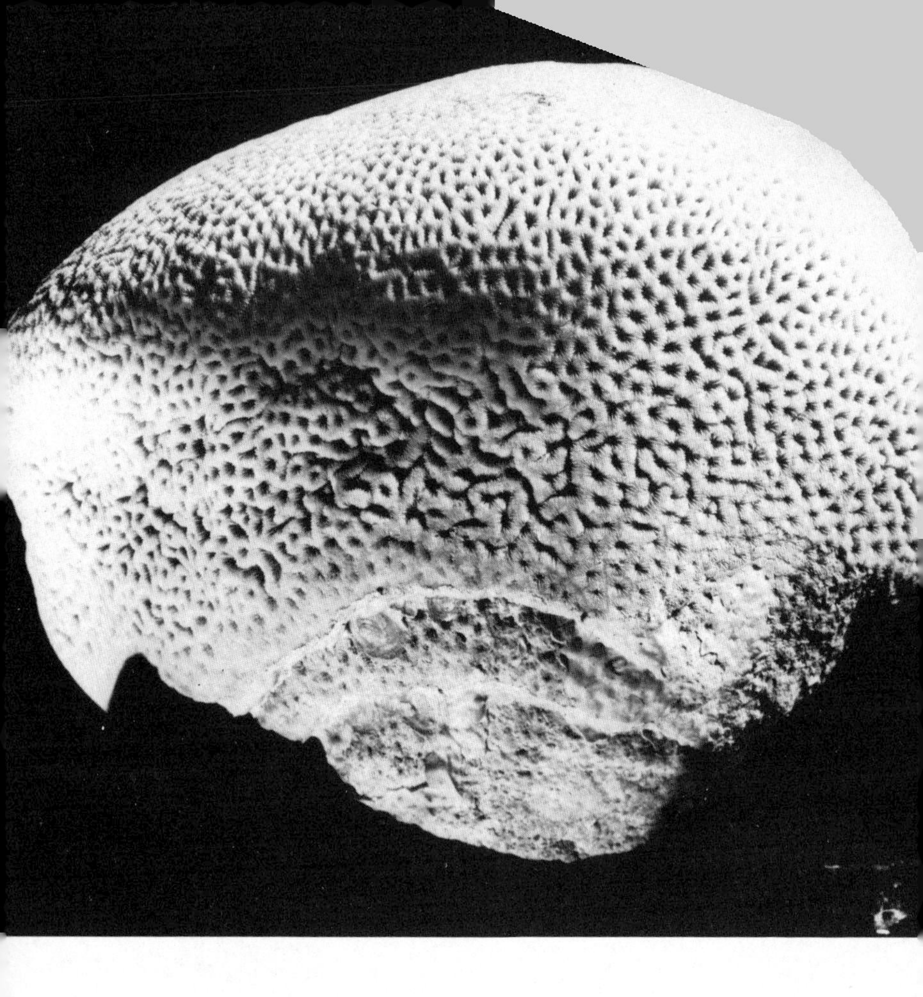

11. Colony of *Siderastrea stellata* Verrill x 1 1/3

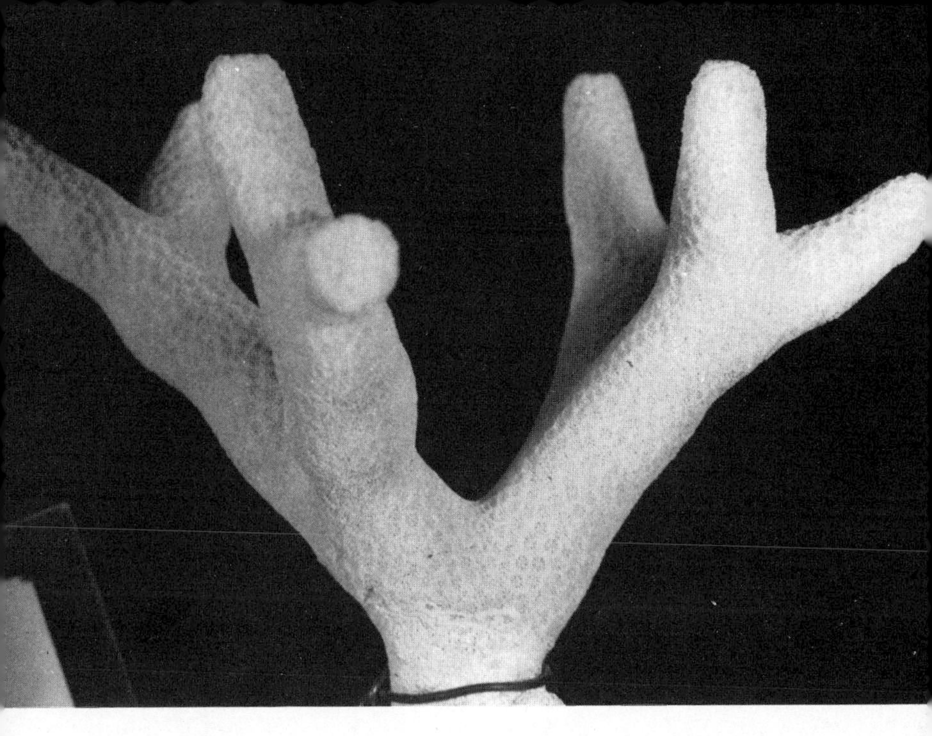

12. Portion of branch of *Porites furcata* Lamarck x 1 1/3 M.L. 8.11

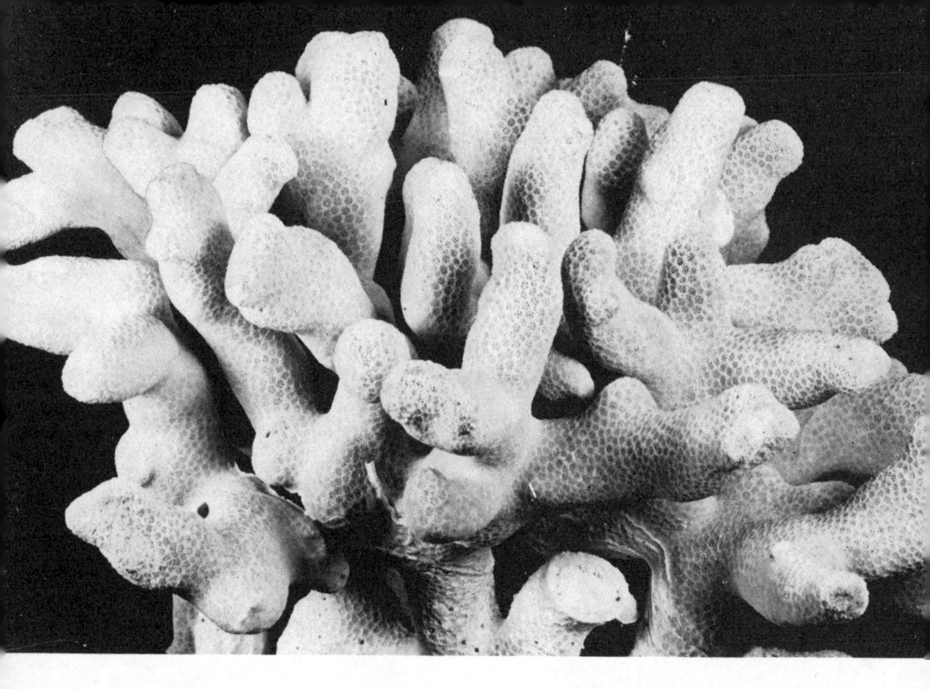

13. Branching colony of *Porites porites* (Pallas) x 8 5/8 M.L. 8.9

14. Surface of *Porites porites* (Pallas) x 14 M.L. 8.9

15. Surface of *Porites astreoides* Lamarck x 12 3/4 M.L. 8.14

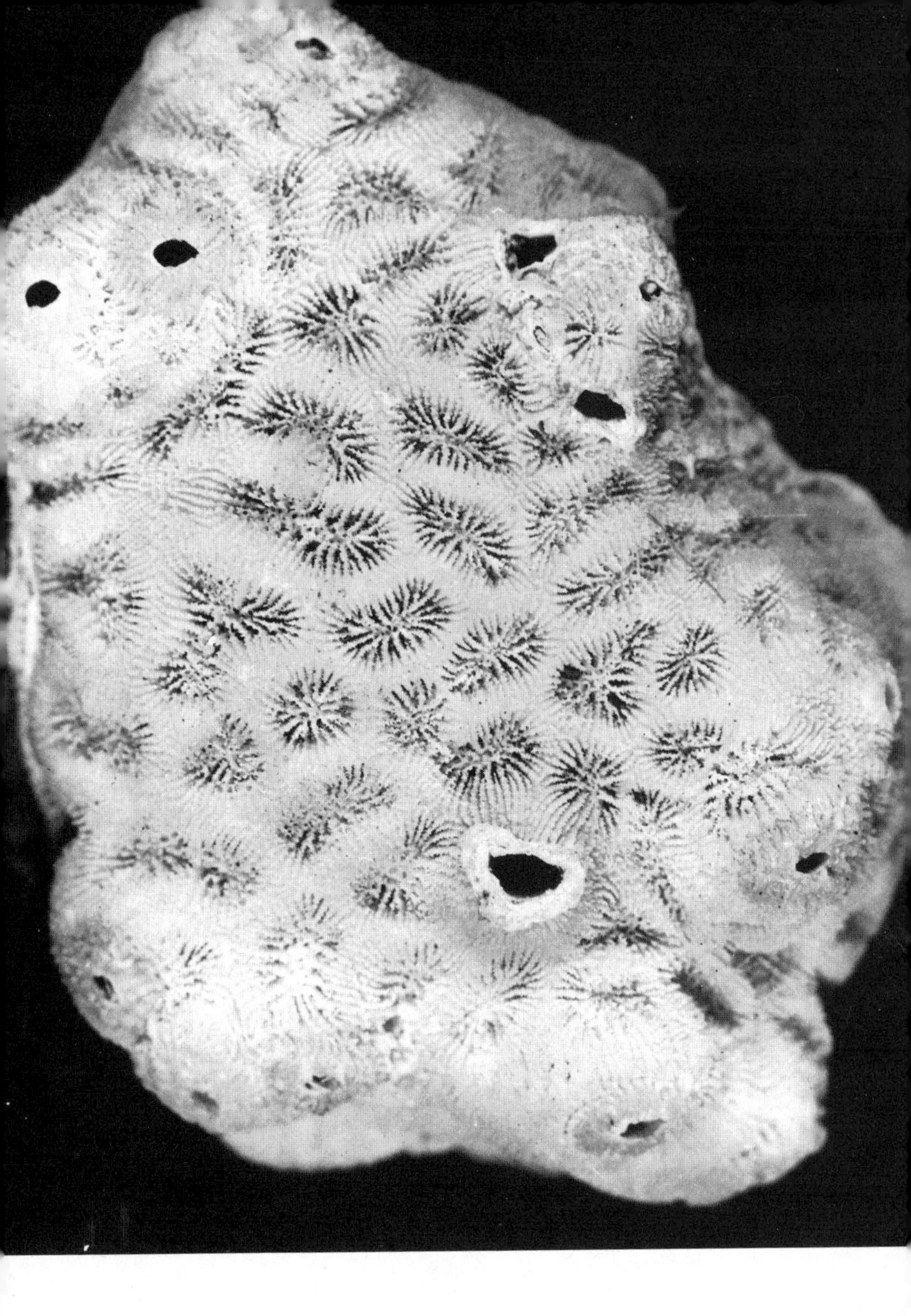

16. Encrusting growth of *Favia fragum* (Esper) x 2 7/8 M.L. 8.35

17. Surface of *Favia fragum* (Esper) x 9 M.L. 8.35

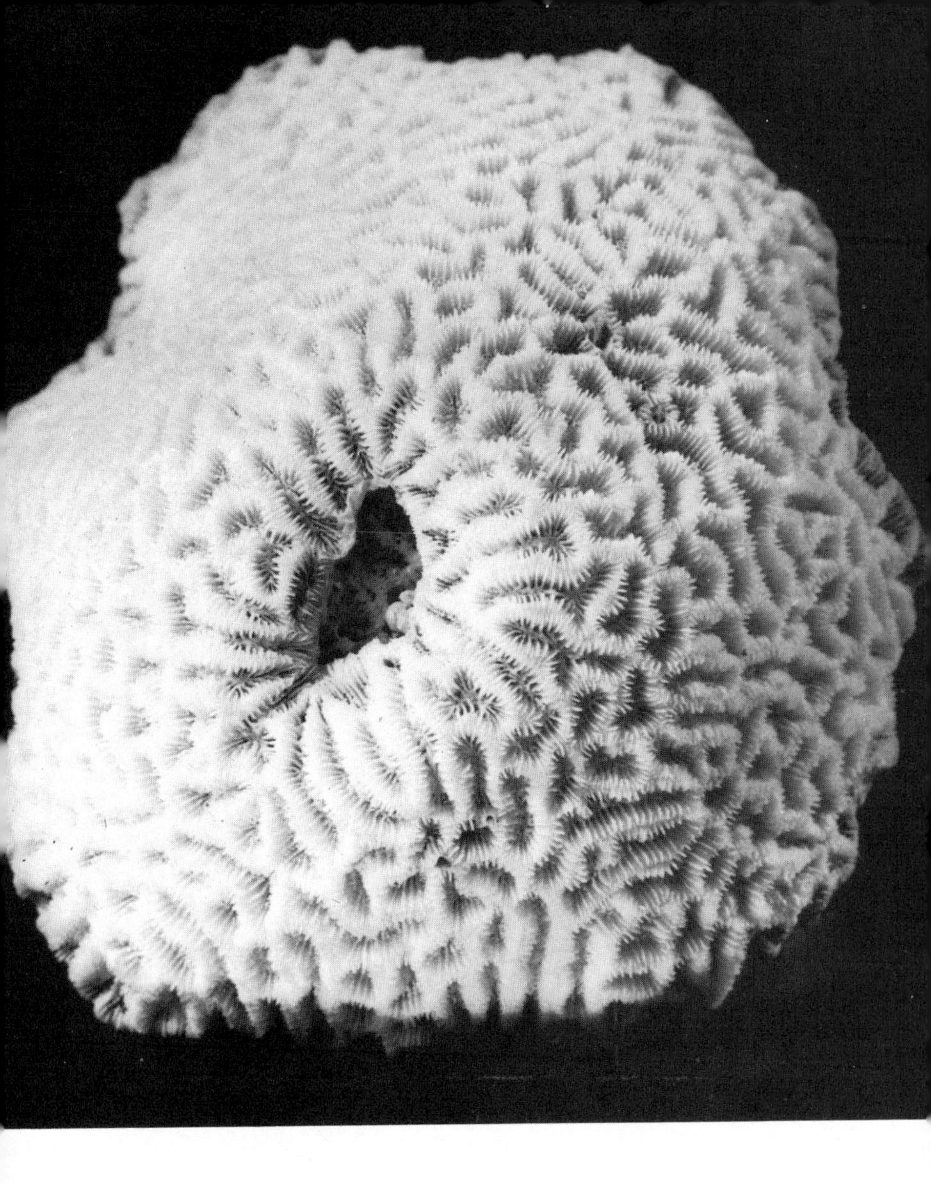

18. Colony of *Favia conferta* Verrill x 3/4

19. Portion of colony of *Diploria clivosa* (Ellis and Solander) x 9/16 M.L. 8.51

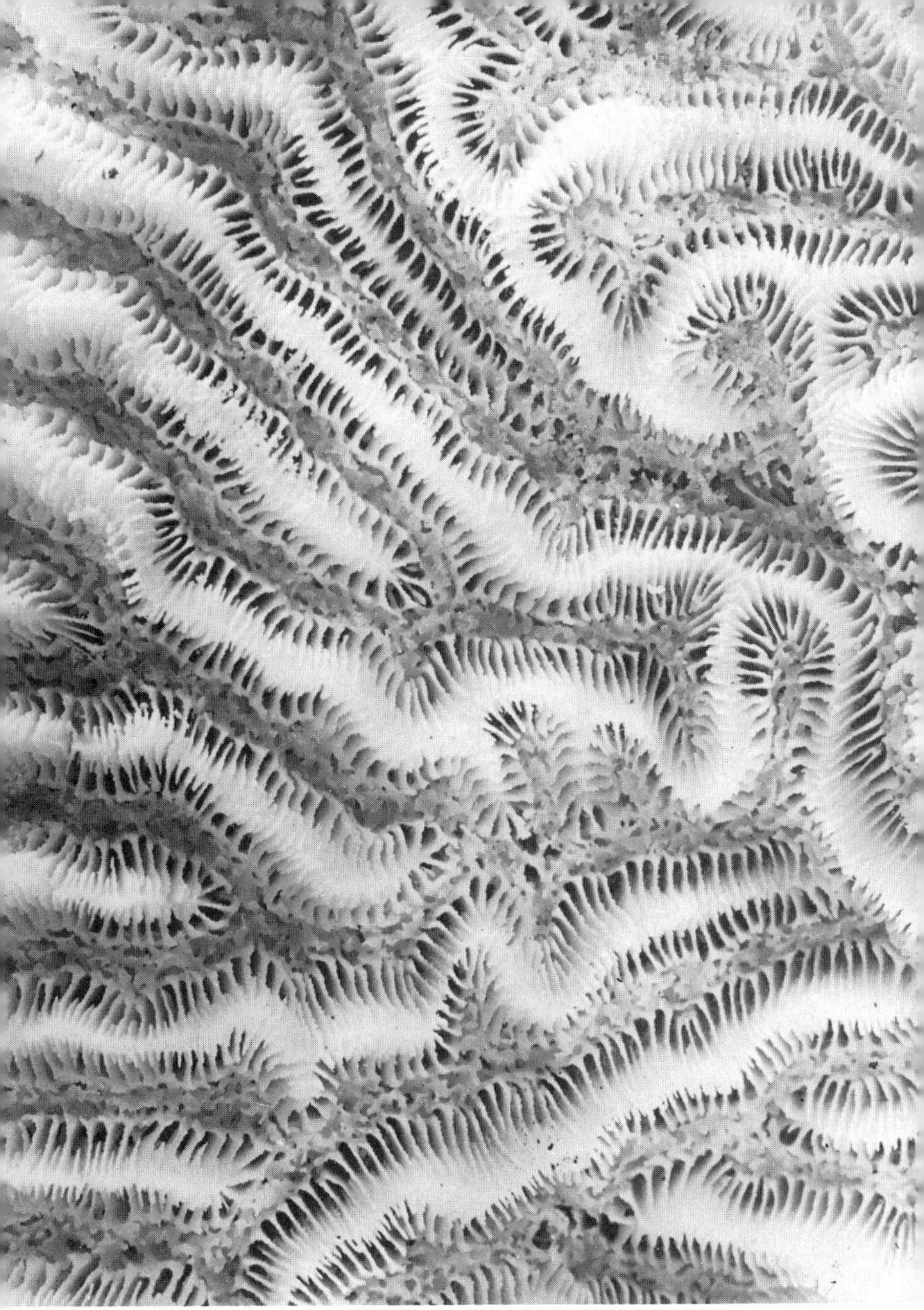

20. Surface of *Diploria clivosa* (Ellis and Solander) 2 2/3
M.L. 8.112

21. Surface of *Diploria labyrinthiformis* (Linnaeus) x 4 M.L. 8.116

22. Surface of *Diploria strigosa* (Dana) x 4 M.L. 8.52

23. Surface of *Colpophyllia natans* (Houttuyn) . x 13 1/3 M.L. 8.103

24. Colony of *Colpophyllia amaranthus* (Houttuyn) x 1 2/3

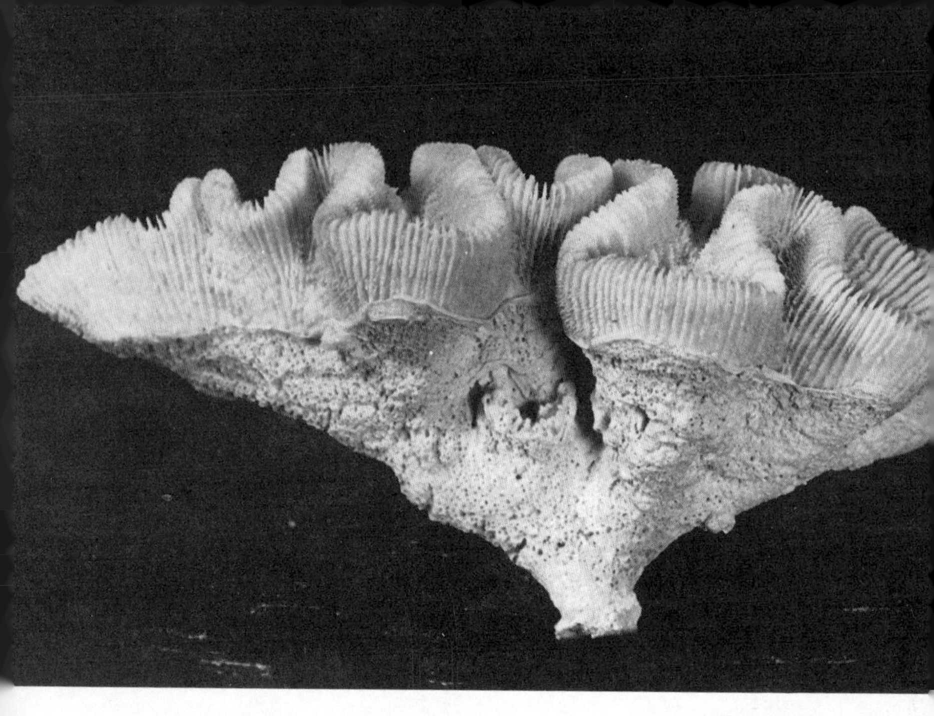

25. *Manicina areolata* (Linnaeus) viewed from the side x 1 1/3
M.L. 8.134

26. *Manicina areolata* (Linnaeus) viewed from above x 1 5/8
M.L. 8.134

27. Surface of *Manicina areolata* (Linnaeus) x 4 M.L. 8.45

28. Colony of *Cladocora arbuscula* Lesueur x 1 7/8 M.L. 8.24

29. Colony of *Solenastrea hyades* (Dana) x 1 3/8 M.L. 8.31

30. Surface of *Solenastrea hyades* (Dana) x 9 M.L. 8.31

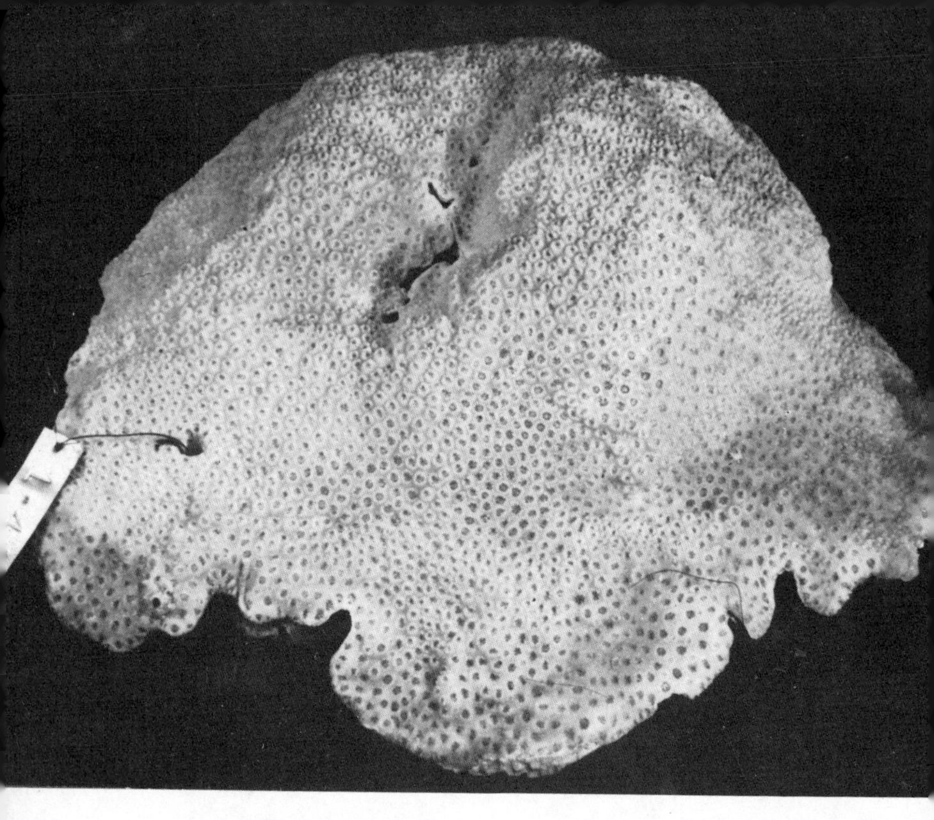

31. Colony of *Montastrea annularis* (Ellis and Solander) x 1/2
M.L. 8.41

32. Surface of *Montastrea annularis* (Ellis and Solander) x 13 1/2
M.L. 8.41

33. Surface of *Montastrea cavernosa* (Linnaeus) x 14 M.L. 8.34

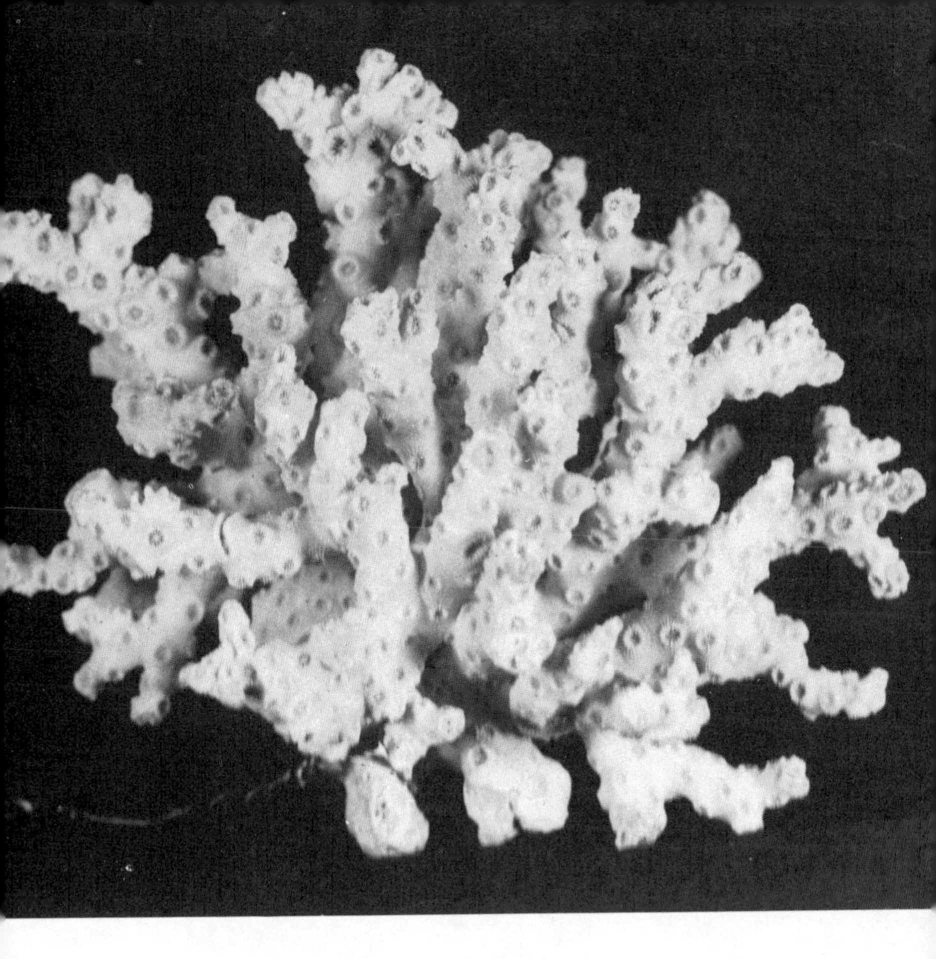

34. Colony of *Oculina diffusa* Lamarck x 1 1/8 M.L. 8.26

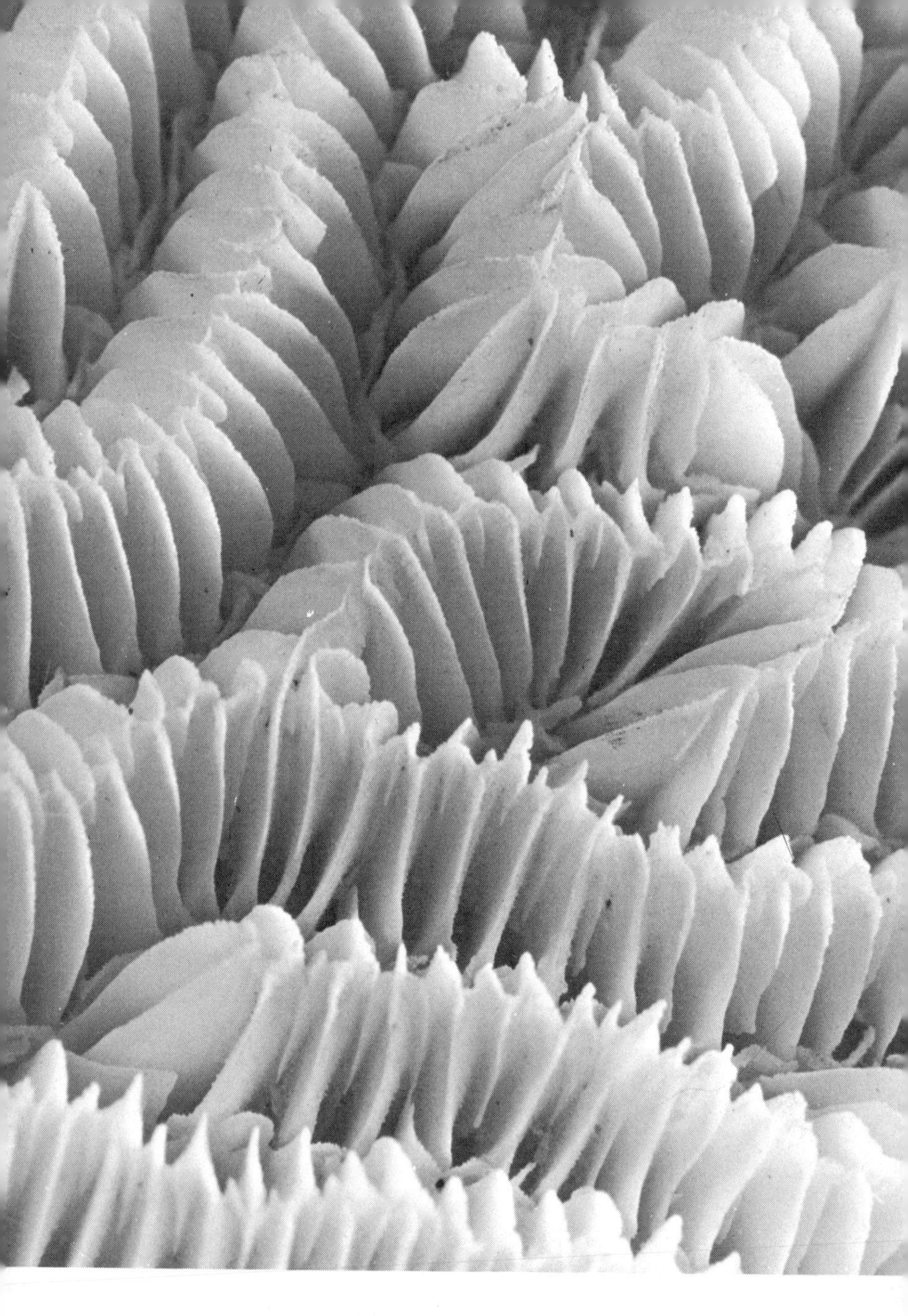

35. Surface of *Meandrina meandrites* (Linnaeus) x 4 M.L. 8.48

36. Colony of *Meandrina brasiliensis* (Edwards and Haime) x 1 1/4
Frank Lyman

37. Surface of *Dichocoenia stokesii* Edwards and Haime x 14
M.L. 8.38

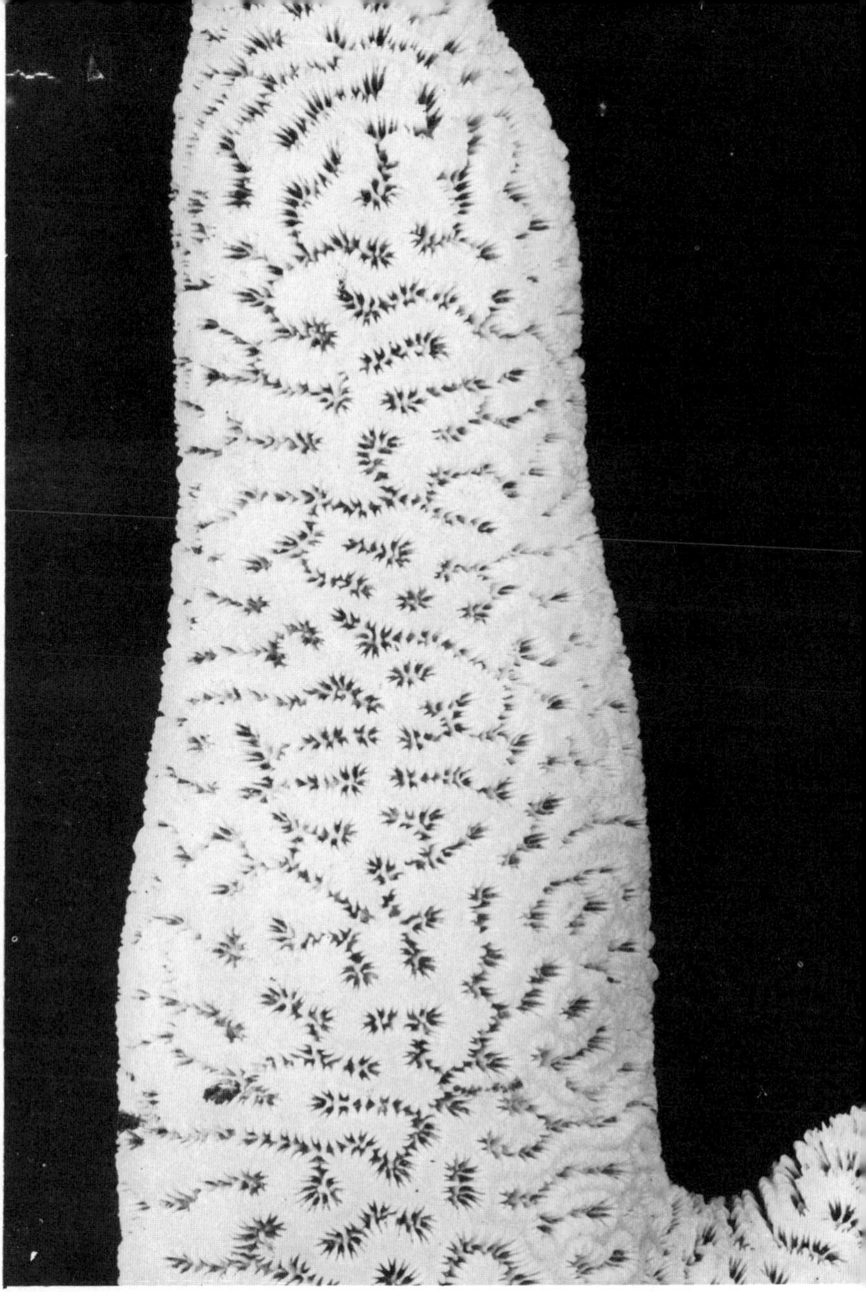

38. Part of a colony of *Dendrogyra cylindrus* Ehrenberg x 1 3/8
M.L. 8.50

39. Surface of *Dendrogyra cylindrus* Ehrenberg x 3 1/3 M.L. 8.50

40. Colony of *Mussismilia harttii* (Verrill) x 1 1/2

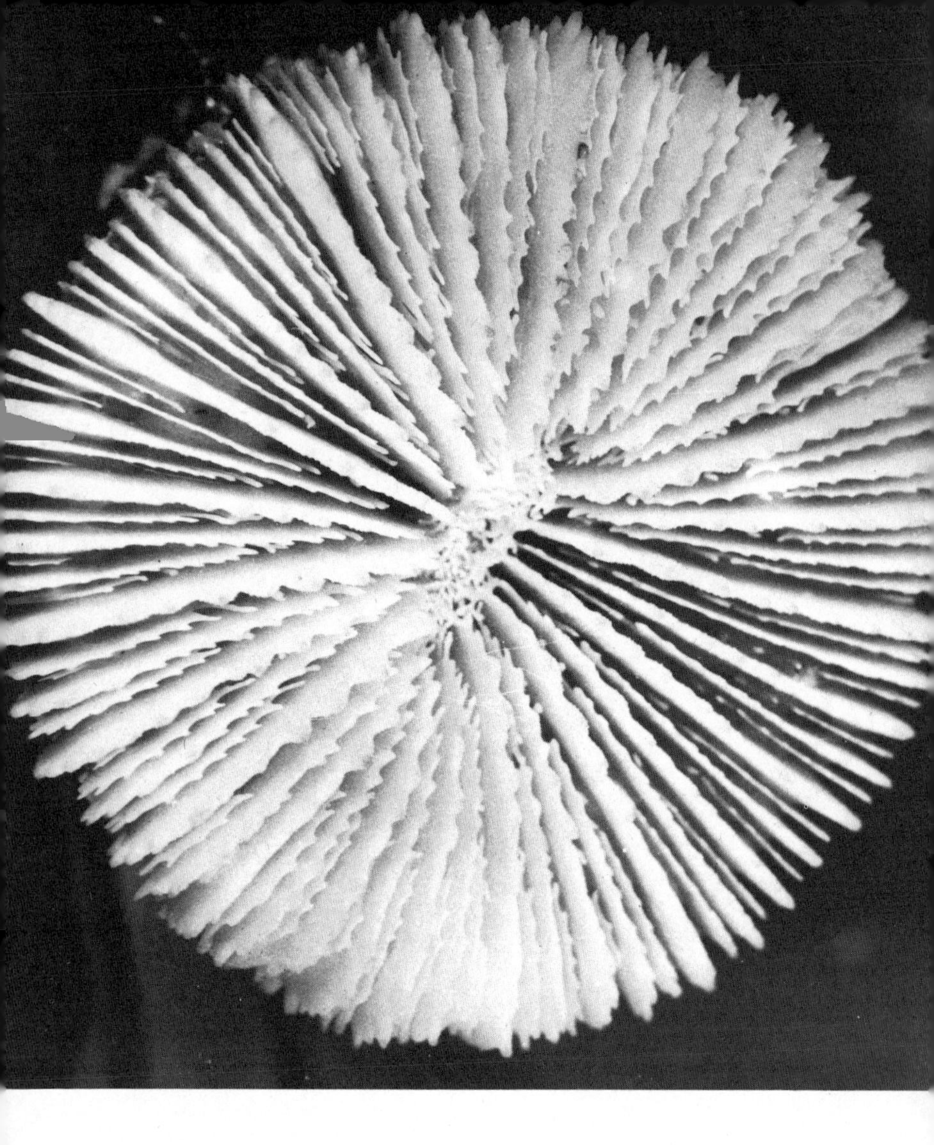

41. *Scolymia lacera* (Pallas) x 3/4 M.L. 8.50

42. Colony of *Mussa angulosa* (Pallas) x 3/4 M.L. 9.85

43. Surface of *Isophyllastrea rigida* (Dana) x 3 1/2 M.L. 8.105

44. Colony of *Mycetophyllia lamarckiana* (Edwards and Haime) x 1
M.L. 8.126

45. Surface of *Mycetophyllia lamarckiana* (Edwards and Haime) x 2 1/2 M.L. 8.97

46. Surface of *Isophyllia sinuosa* var *fragilis* x2 1/2 M.L. 8.101

47. Surface of *Isophyllia multiflora* Verrill x 4 M.L. 8.42

48. Colony of *Eusmilia fastigiata* (Pallas) x 1 1/3 M.L. 8.27

Index